SAP DEVELOPERS GUIDE TO PHP
2nd Edition

CRAIG CMEHIL

ISBN-13: 978-1493514748

ISBN-10: 1493514741

First Edition
ISBN 1-59229-066-3

SAP Press is an imprint of Galileo Press.
Fort Lee (NJ), USA
Bonn, Germany

Editor Stefan Proksch
Copy Editor Nancy Etscovitz, UCG, Inc., Boston, MA
Cover Design Vera Brauner
Printed in Germany

DEDICATION

To those who have found and follow their path.

CONTENTS

FORWARD

Due to the growing interest in the development of solutions in a corporate environment at reduced costs, PHP is becoming increasingly more popular. The need for quick and simple guides to help developers and their employers get started, however, is problematic. PHP has many such guides that are available and easy to locate; for those of you working within the SAP environment, the information you need is readily accessible from multiple sources as well. What is lacking is what happens when two such technologies come together.

You have two distinct groups of people, developers in this case, who have little or no connection with one another. And here, as in other cases, connections are created out of patience and understanding. Whether you're a seasoned SAP developer or a developer just getting started, with the proper understanding and a few easy examples, you can build this connection.

Our goal in this book is to try to remove some of the guesswork in order to strengthen the ties between SAP and PHP, until we finally have a solid connection.

We do not intend to teach you how to program or how to work with ABAP or other SAP technologies; rather, we hope to show you how you can use PHP to read, display, and access the different types of SAP systems .

The original version of this book was published in 2006 by SAP Press a Galileo Press publication and was part of the "SAP Essentials" a set of books designed and targeted to SAP developers and the developer community.

Fast forward to 2013, as the original book is no longer being published I contacted SAP PRESS and asked if it would be OK to take my original content and republish it again as demand has been increasing for copies of the book. They agreed and so I undertook the task of creating a new version of the book. The content has remained the same so if you purchased the original in the past you will find that you have the same book - it just looks slightly different.

INTRODUCTION TO PHP

The History

In the Fall of 1994, Rasmus Lerdorf created what would later become known as the PHP programming language. Used almost entirely by Lerdorf for the tracking of information on his own home page, PHP (known then as "Personal Home Page Tools") was very limited in its capabilities, which were based primarily on Perl [1] scripts. The originally version of PHP which is still available today via, from http://museum.php.net and is only 26 kilobytes in size. As Lerdorf required more capabilities, he moved on to create PHP/FI or Personal Home Page Tools/Form Interpreter, which was a C implementation that allowed for database interaction and dynamic web page building. In 1995, Lerdorf provided the source code of PHP/FI to the world for code improvements and bug fixes.

PHP's future really began to solidify with the release of PHP/FI 2.0 in November of 1997. With an estimated following of thousands of users worldwide and approximately 1% of the domains on the Internet having it installed, PHP/FI 2.0 took the next big step—it was upgraded to PHP 3.0.

While working on an eCommerce University project, Andi Gutmans and Zeev Suraski found PHP/FI 2.0 to be lacking and decided to rewrite the entire package. To build on the existing user base of PHP/FI and in a show of cooperation, Suraski and Gutmans joined Lerdorf and announced PHP 3.0 to be the next official release, thus halting the development of PHP/FI 2.0.

With public testing of PHP 3.0 underway since its launch in June of 1998, Suraski and Gutmans began to rewrite the core of PHP. This rewrite produced the Zend Engine, and the two moved on to found Zend

Technologies[2]. Zend has been present now for ever major advancement of PHP, the latest being PHP 5.0, released on the Zend Engine II on July 13, 2004. PHP is known today as *PHP: Hypertext Preprocessor*, which means that it handles data before it becomes HTML (*Hypertext Markup Language*). As of 17 January 2013, version 5.4.11 was released with Zend Engine 2.0 forming it's core and beginning in the middle of April of 2013 version 5.5 has begun beta testing.

According to Netcraft's April 2002 survey, PHP is now the most deployed server-side scripting language, running on approximately 9 million of the 37 million domains in their survey. This is confirmed by PHP's own figures, which show PHP usage (measured on a per-domain basis) growing at roughly 5% per month. In May 2003, almost 13 million domains were using PHP, based on the same source.[3] Today, the number of domains using PHP is even greater (see Figure 1.1).

PHP is also considered to be one of the few truly cross-platform programming languages, or to be more precise, one of the few truly cross-platform "scripting languages,"[4] because it can run on almost any operating system and can be moved from each operating system with little or no changes to the coding.

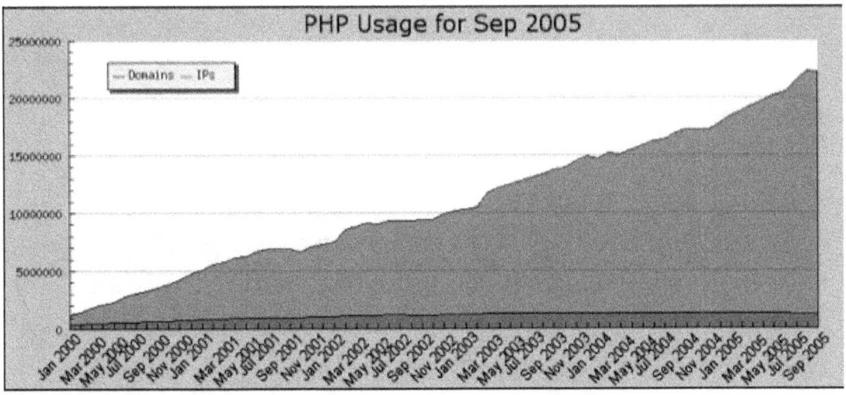

Figure 1.1: PHP Usage Statistics for September 2005

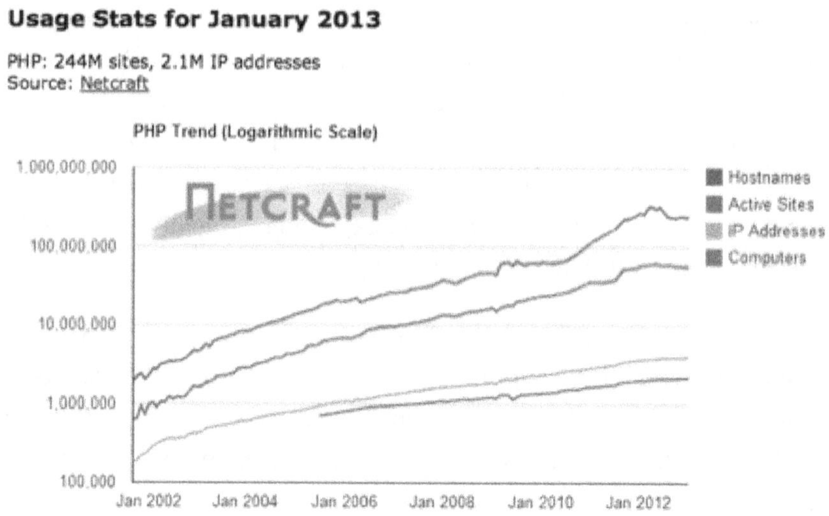

Figure 1.1a: Updated PHP Usage Statistics for January 2013

As you can see from this latest graphic via Netcraft PHP has continued to grow to be one of the leading server side languages available today. Popular platforms such as Wordpress, Joomla and Drupal all are based on PHP with millions of instances of each running world wide.

Why PHP?

Today PHP is one of the most popular server-side scripting languages; however, is that enough to convince someone that this is the optimal platform for development? Some of the reasons that account for PHP's popularity include the following:

It's a loose language, a dynamically typed language, and therefore, the rules aren't as strict with variables—they don't have to be declared, and they can hold any type of object, thereby making PHP an ideal environment for rapid prototyping and development of not only small but large applications (see Table 1.1).

PHP applications can also be both—based as well as desktop style applications via the command line compilers.

Why?	# Responses	Ratio
Easy to develop with	3093	89%
Web application focus	2328	67%
Affordable	2311	66%
Flexibility	2287	66%
Apache integration	2109	61%
Performance	1997	57%
Preference for non-Microsoft technology	1829	53%
Multiple platform support	1785	51%
Availability of the source code (open source)	1404	40%
UNIX/Linux investment	1304	37%
Multiple web	853	25%

server support		
Time to market	606	17%
Inherited an existing PHP system	281	8%
Other, please specify	300	9%

Table 1.1 Zend Technologies PHP Survey Results June 2003

In short, PHP is easier, faster, better, and more flexible to learn than most other languages, as well as being a very adaptable and "forgiving" language in terms of syntax and coding.

Often, it is because of these reasons that PHP is such an optimal tool. Within SAP, a company with so many possibilities for development, there is one area that affects every aspect of a project and that is time. You can use PHP to transform a concept or idea—rapidly develop, deploy, and present it—in a far more visual way than is possible with a presentation. Here, the idea is not to replace defined development methods, but to enhance the conceptual phase of the project, thereby allowing for more freedom in the initial stages. Once the project is well defined, you can begin working through the first stages of development. By using PHP, the value of the project in the initial stages can be quickly, cheaply, and easily determined, saving valuable time and resources. All of this depends on having the ability to work with PHP, which is something anyone who has the desire and the interest can do and learn well enough for these purposes.

How PHP Works

How PHP works is actually quite simple and easy to understand: The client machine will send the request to the server, usually in the form of a URL (*Uniform Resource Locator*) that will then be taken by the server and sent to the appropriate compiler, which will, in return, send the result back to the client machine. Figure 1.2 shows the process from the client request via a URL to the server that processes the PHP and returns HTML to the client.

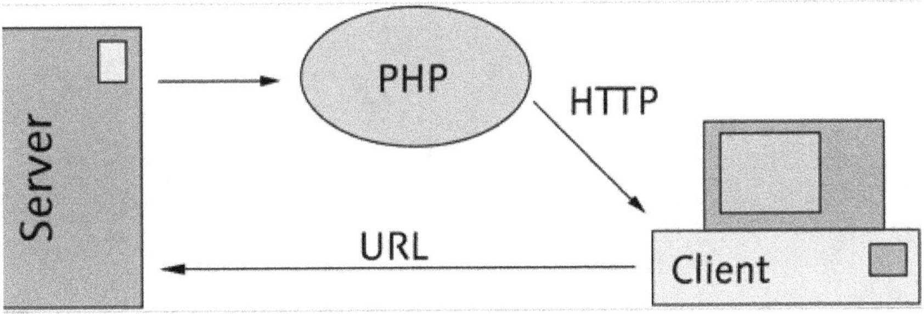

Figure 1.2: PHP Process

This is a standard server-side processing model. Next, the result that the client machine receives is interpreted by the browser and the HTML code is displayed appropriately in the browser window.

For example, let's take this example:

http://localhost:8080/image.php.

This is the URL that our browser will call. The server will locate this URL and verify that the extension has been defined as a PHP extension and therefore route the request to the PHP compiler.

The compiler will now interpret this request and load the *image.php* file (see Listing 1.1), read each line of the file, and determine what actions to take.

```
<?php

$image =
"http://static.php.net/www.php.net/images/php.gif";

?>

<html>

<head>

<title>image.php example</title>

</head>

<body>

<? echo "<img src=\"$image\" border=\"0\"> "; ?>

</body>

</html>
```

Listing 1.1: Sample image.php Page

As you can see in Listing 1.1, there's a mix of HTML and PHP on the page. The PHP compiler compiles the items on this page that must be compiled, that is, the items between the "<?" and "?>" that indicate embedded PHP code. Of course, this is just a simplified example to show you how PHP works. What we have done here is taken a variable called $image and assigned it the URL location of a graphic file that we want to display. This is considered a "simplified example," because you could have just as easily provided the location instead of the $image and therefore saved a processing step.

After the server has compiled the PHP code, the results are returned to the client in the form of static HTML (see Figure 1.3).

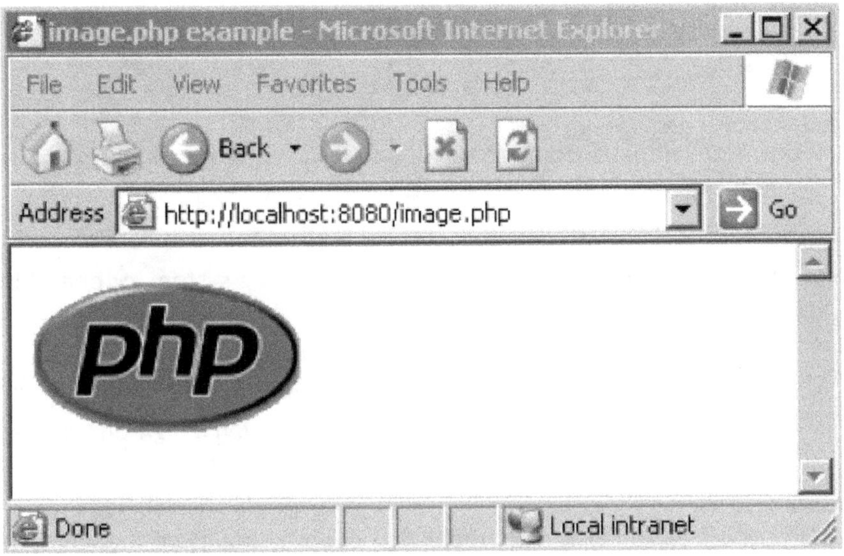

Figure 1.3: Result of Compiled PHP Code and HTML Code

If you now reviewed the source code of this page, you would no longer see any of our PHP coding, only the compiled and static HTML (see Figure 1.4).

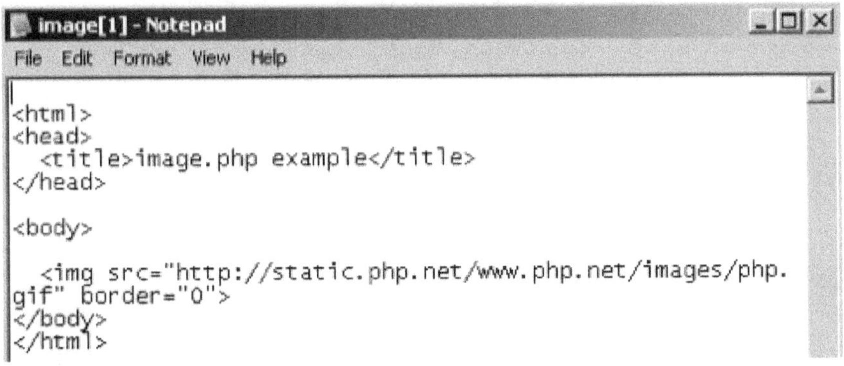

Figure 1.4: Source Code of New Compiled Page

The Basics of Getting Started

From a developer's point of view, you'll need two basic items to get started—the desire to work with PHP and the means to do so. The latter can be something as basic as a simple text editor such as Notepad or WordPad that comes with the Windows operating system, or one of the various editors that come with the different flavors of Linux.

Or, you can try one of the more powerful development environments such as Eclipse with the various PHP plugins, or even a high-end package like the *Zend Studio* from Zend Technologies.

Whichever editor or environment you choose should be fine. Working with PHP is similar to working with HTML, or any other programming language for that matter, and the tool is most often not critical. What matters is that you employ whatever you need to get the job done.

For SAP developers, if you have already deployed and started using the SAP NetWeaver Developer Studio, I would highly recommend using "PHP-eclipse,"[5] which is a plugin for the Eclipse IDE. This plugin is easily integrated into Eclipse and quite handy when working with PHP.

SAPRFC and Environment

A Merging of Technologies

You have SAP installed and a strong ABAP presence. Now you need a fast and easy way to deploy data into a web environment, and, of course, be able to do so as cost-effectively as possible.

SAP already has some powerhouse tools for connecting Java,[1] as well as Microsoft's own *.NET* environment. There are also many tools like Eclipse[2] and those from SUN and Oracle that are free to use. You may ask, "If they're free, why not use them?" Well, generally, this is a safe recommendation, however, for a powerful and stable environment, companies tend to want the higher end packages, because they assume these tools are stronger and more stable. Although this is not always true, neither is it always false.

For example, most companies moving to a Java environment tend to deploy servers such as *IBM WebSphere* or *BEA Logic*, thus replacing the savings they made in their development environments with high-end costs in production. In this way, .NET is similar, except for the fact that you have fewer savings in the development stage and you're locked into a particular platform.

So again you might ask, "Why PHP?" Well, it's cross-platform, free, and requires only the addition of an HTTP server. The HTTP server is present in a Windows server, or easily added to any environment for virtually no cost, except the time required to add it, if you choose the Apache HTTP Server, for example.

Another main reason for choosing PHP is because of a little "free" package that I came across on the Internet. *SAPRFC* is an extension of PHP 4.0 and PHP 5.0 that allows for the interaction of ABAP and PHP, similar to how *Java Connector* (JCo) allows for the interaction of Java and ABAP.

SAPRFC was registered on SourceForge.net—an online collaboration environment for development projects (http://sourceforge.net)—in June of 2001, and has shown a steady activity (see Figure 2.1) since its inception.

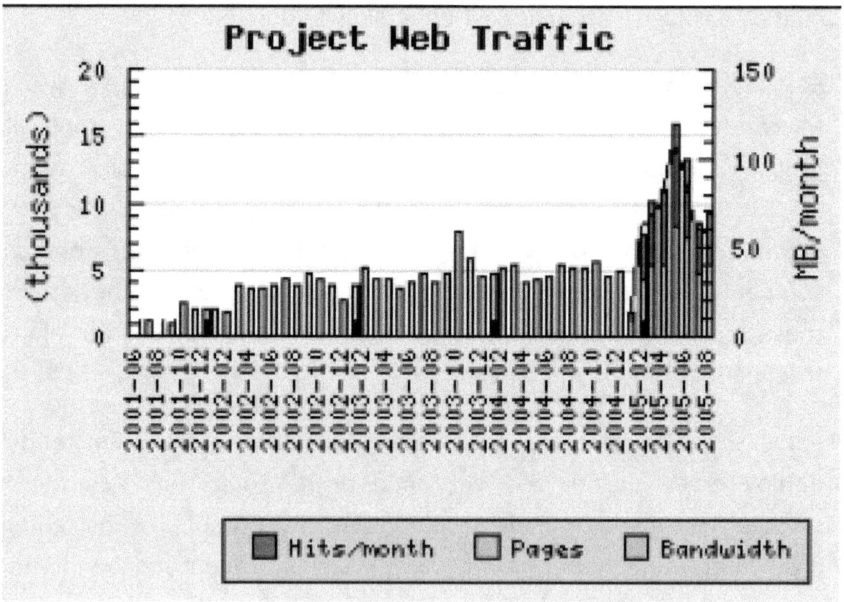

Figure 2.1: Statistics for SAPRFC Extension for PHP (Web Traffic)

Even more exciting is the steady increase in updates, the latest at the time of the writing of this book, which appeared in August 23, 2005 as Release 1.4. As you can see in Figure 2.2, as updates go, so do downloads.

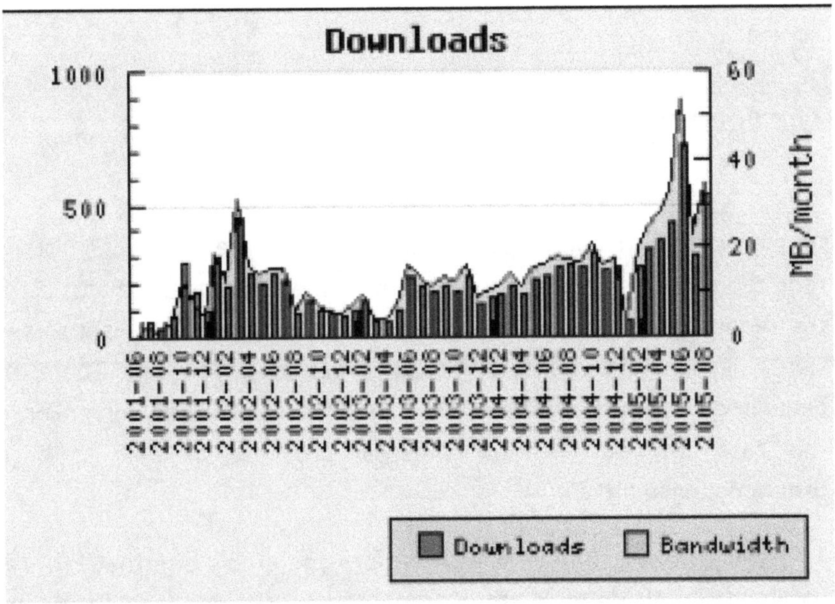

Figure 2.2: Statistics for SAPRFC Extension for PHP (Downloads)

Some of you will still need the older version of the SAPRFC library which is still available via SourceForge however for newer releases of the Wrapper we have to jump to 2009 when Piers Harding, http://www.piersharding.com/blog/, agreed to take over development together with direct contact with the SAP RFCSDK development group.

Piers keeps in contact with the community via a discussion thread within the SAP Community Network (SCN), that link is http://scn.sap.com/thread/1208671 and the entire project itself can be found via GitHub .

https://github.com/piersharding/php-sapnwrfc

For the most part implementation is the same regardless it's just that you will need to ensure that you match SAPRFC version and SAP GUI library versions.

The Environment

As mentioned previously (see Section 1.4), for the developer, little is required in terms of software to work with, which means that most of the requirements are on the server. Considering that PHP is a server-side language, this makes sense. However, don't despair. There are actually only three items that you need to set up on the server, or, in this case, on your local machine, in order to be able to begin programming in PHP.

To begin with, you'll need a web server—preferably one that PHP can easily communicate with—then, you'll need PHP itself, and finally, the SAPRFC module.

To get started I have chosen the Apache HTTP Server, primarily because it's well supported, heavily used, easy to connect with PHP, and free. Apache HTTP Server is an Open Source project[3] and most likely, it is the server you'll find deployed within your production environment.

Warning

You will need to check the SAPRFC website to ensure that you download a version of Apache HTTP Server and a version of PHP that will work together.

http://saprfc.sourceforge.net

https://github.com/piersharding/php-sapnwrfc

HTTP Server

Once you have downloaded the install package for the Apache HTTP Server, you can then do the standard install. Note that even when you follow the standard installation of the Apache HTTP Server, there can be slight deviations in the names that are displayed in Figure 2.3.

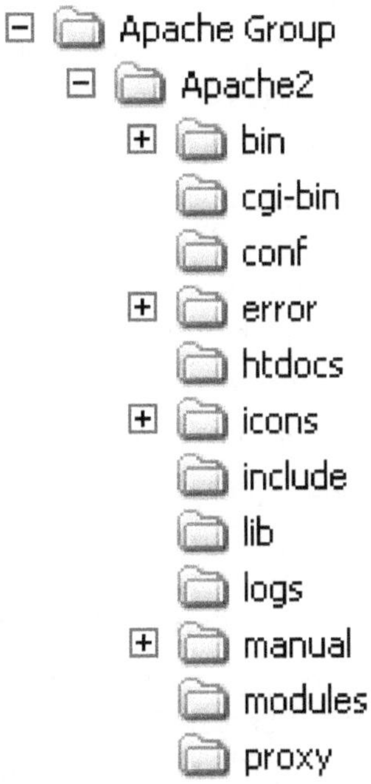

Figure 2.3: Apache HTTP Server Directory Structure

Now that we have an HTTP server installed, we will need to make some configuration changes to ensure that it works properly.

The main configuration file for the Apache HTTP Server is located in the *conf* subdirectory and is called *httpd.conf*. This is the file that you need to open and look at; opening it with a standard text editor will suffice.

Each of the items that we are going to change are well documented in the configuration file and easily found by doing a simple search in the document. The first item that we are going to look at is the "ServerRoot". This is the location that the Apache HTTP Server was installed at, and this is the location that needs to be changed if you decide to move the directory to a new location.

The next item is "Listen", which you can set to 80 or 8080 after the standard install. This item is actually the port number of your computer/server where the Apache HTTP Server will listen and react to requests from a web browser. Each computer/server has ports ranging from 1 to 65535; several have standard definitions recognized throughout the world, others are considered to be for temporary communications. Other computer/servers can access these ports for information exchange; 80 and 8080 are defined as the standard ports for HTTP traffic. Let's use 8080 for our installation.

The next item is the "DocumentRoot", which is the home of the webpage or website. This is where we will store, edit, and work with all of our pages and scripts. This item can be changed to any directory on your computer/server that you choose. For our purposes, we'll leave it as the default location of *htdocs* under the Apache HTTP Server directory.

Now to try it out, load your favorite web browser and type the following into the address location: "http://localhost:8080". "localhost" is the local computer/server running the Apache HTTP Server. The resulting page should then look something like Figure 2.4. If this is successful, we're ready to go onto the next step.

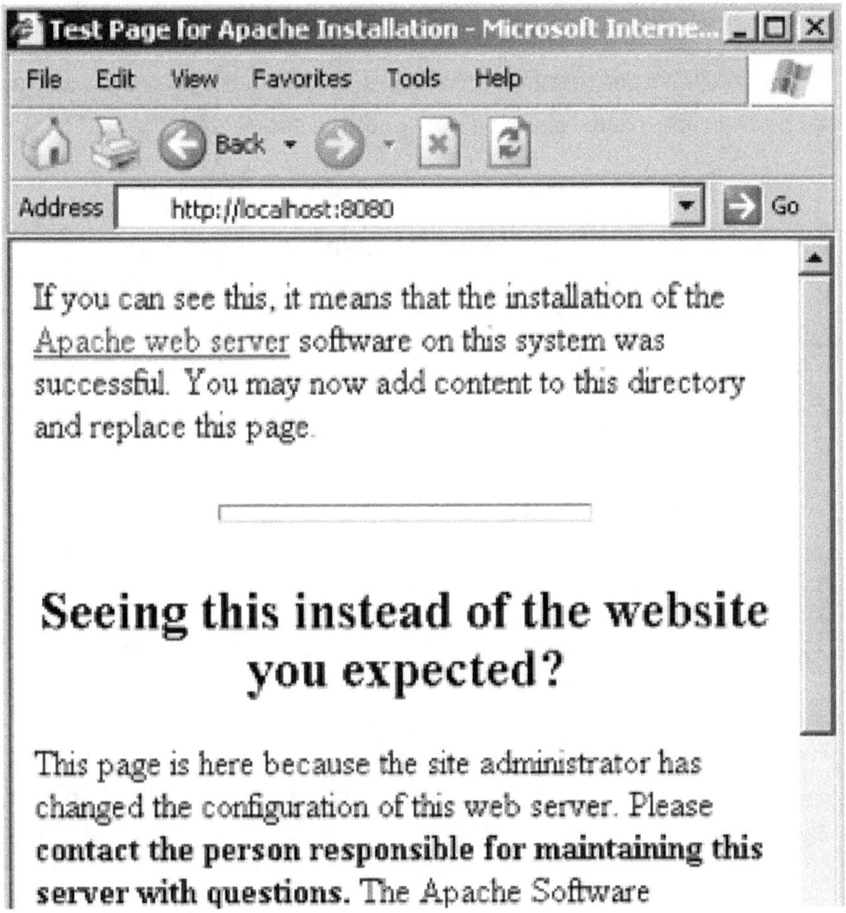

Figure 2.4: Default Resulting Page

If you do not see a page similar to Figure 2.4, then it is possible that your web server has not been properly started. If you choose to have only the server run when started manually, you'll need to execute the apache.exe[4] file located in the *bin* subdirectory itself. Your resulting URL will then be *http://localhost:8080* or an additional port number that you have manually specified under "Listen" in the *httpd.conf* file. The results, however, should be the same.

Now to get a little more familiar with how the Apache HTTP Server works, we are going to create a very simple and easy *index.html* page inside of our *htdocs* subdirectory.

Open your favorite text or WYSIWYG editor (“*What you see is what you get*”) and type in the following HTML source code (see Listing 2.1).

```
<!DOCTYPE html PUBLIC "-//W3C//DTD XHTML 1.0
Transitional//EN"
"http://www.w3.org/TR/xhtml1/DTD/xhtml1-
transitional.dtd">

<html>

<head>

   <title>SAP Developer's Guide to PHP</title>

</head>

<body>

  <h1>SAP Developer's Guide to PHP</h1>

  <img src="sap_developers_guide_php.gif" alt="SAP
Developer's Guide to PHP">

</body>

</html>
```

Listing 2.1   HTML Text for New Index Page

To see code that adheres more to web standards, go to the W3C website at *http://www.w3.org*. The new resulting page in our browser window now shows our changes to *index.html* (see Figure 2.5).

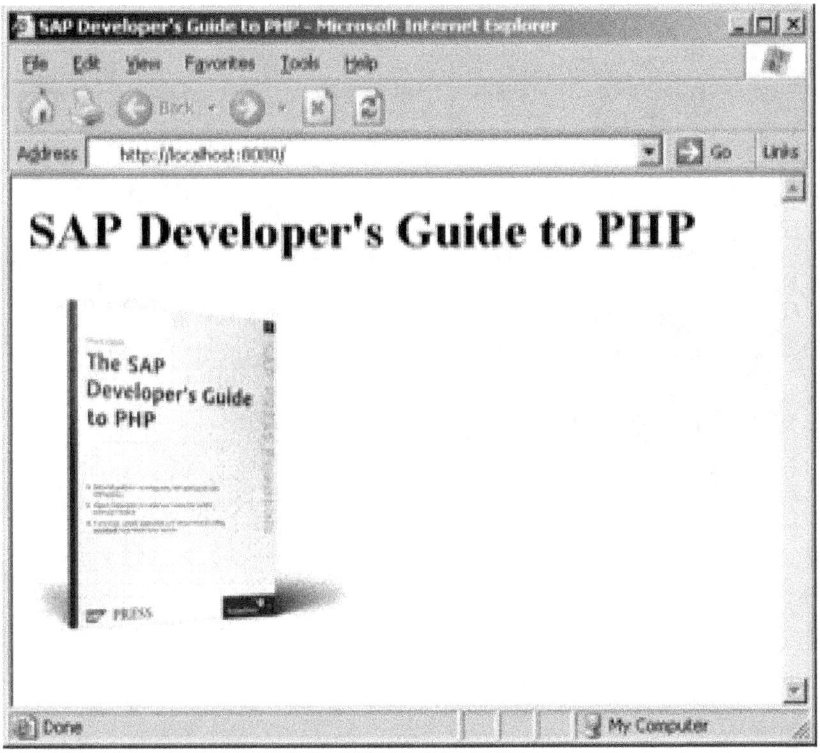

Figure 2.5: New Home Page

Installing PHP

Now that our HTTP server is in place and working, it's time to install PHP. In order to get the download package for PHP, you'll need to go to the PHP website at *http://www.php.net* and select **downloads**. Check the SAPRFC website before to determine which version is necessary.

Once you have the installer downloaded, simply double-click on it to start the process. Here, I've downloaded PHP 4.4.0 (see Figure 2.6).

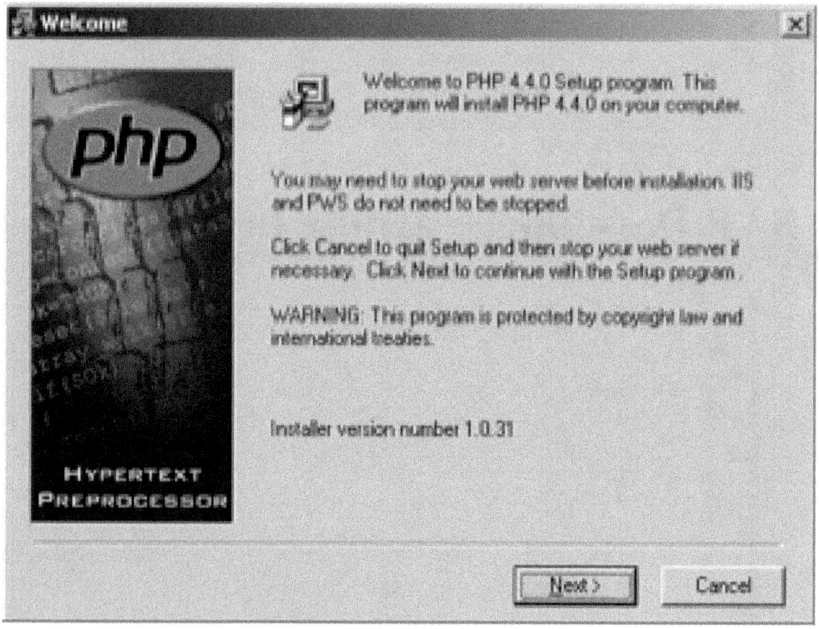

Figure 2.6: PHP Setup Program

With most items, there is always a license, even if it's free, so ensure that you read the license agreement that comes with PHP. Click on the **I Agree** button.

To make life easier, we'll choose the **Advanced** setup option. The reason for this is that we can then set up PHP to be installed as a subdirectory under our Apache HTTP Server, thus making things a bit more compact and later transportable if needed. Click on the **Next** button.

Now select the location to install PHP. First, you should browse to your Apache Group folder, then to Apache2, and then enter "PHP" as the destination. Note that again these names may vary. Click on the **Next** button.

Next, you must back up your files during the install to ensure that you have a smooth uninstall at a later date (see Figure 2.7). This is always helpful and the importance of making a backup cannot be stressed enough! Choose **Yes**, and click on the **Next** button.

Figure 2.7: Backup Replaced Files

The next item of the installer is important for data handling and session handling to make our PHP applications more robust in features and capabilities. Session data will allow us to create more robust - applications including user logins and multiple user logins. I recommend that you simply keep the default locations here for these directories.

Eventually, email always comes into play when creating applications. With PHP, you can now define your email host, SMTP[5] (*Simple Mail Transfer Protocol*) host, and admin email address (see Figure 2.8). Click on the **Next** button.

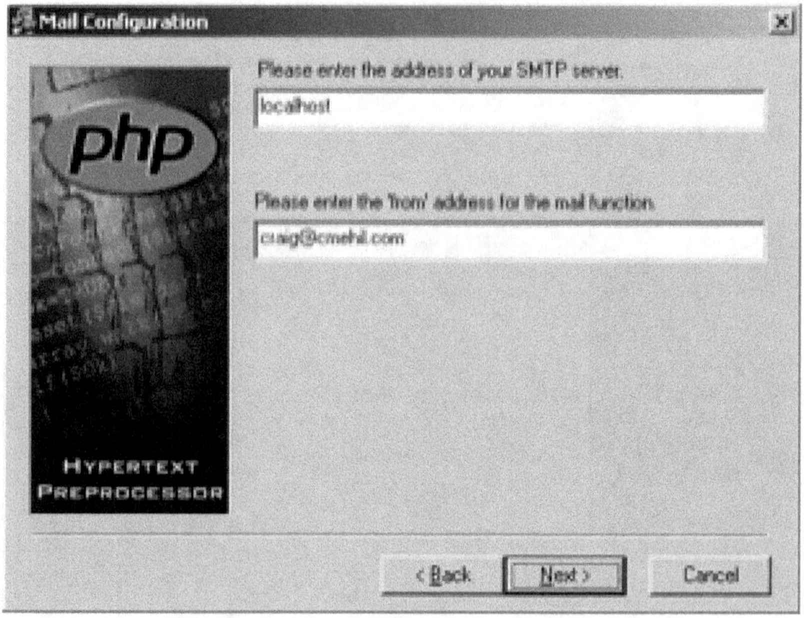

Figure 2.8: SMTP Server Settings

The next item in the wizard that you should pay special attention to is error reporting. By default, the option recommended for development is already selected and should remain as is in our development environment. You may elect to change this option at a later time. It is located in the main configuration file for PHP. Click on the **Next** button.

Earlier (see Section 2.3, HTTP Server) I mentioned that I have chosen to use the Apache HTTP Server here, because it's supported and heavily used. This choice will make installing PHP and connecting it to our HTTP Server that much easier (see Figure 2.9).

However, if you're not using Apache and you've chosen IIS from Microsoft, for example, you should select the appropriate menu option, or read the accompanying documentation that addresses the installation. If the documentation does not cover your HTTP Server of choice, you should contact the support associated with your server and check whether methods for the integration are supported. Click on the **Next** button.

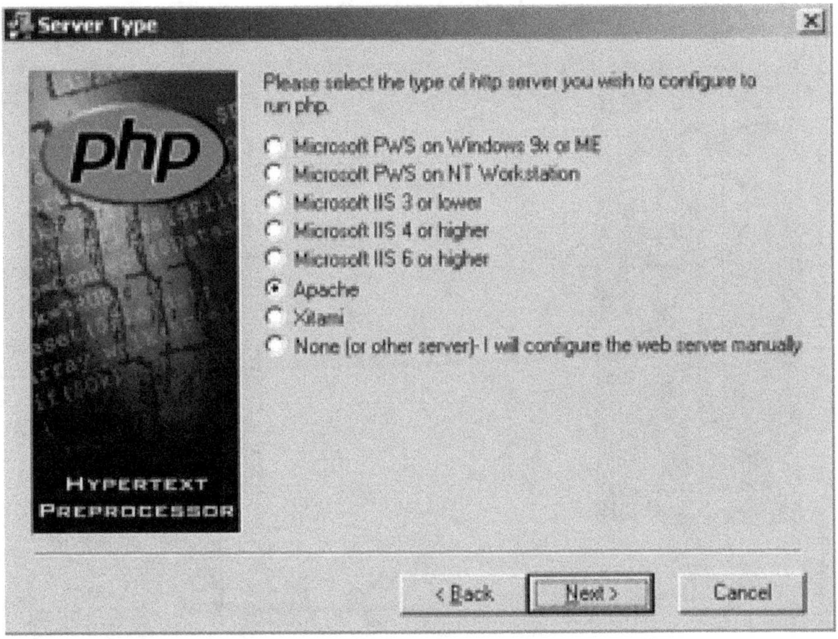

Figure 2.9: Integrating PHP into Apache HTTP Server

Since we are starting fresh with PHP 4 and theoretically this is our first attempt at installing PHP, we can omit using the deprecated PHP extensions from our install (see Figure 2.10). Click on the **Next** button.

With a final click on the **Next** button, we are now ready to install PHP 4.4.0.

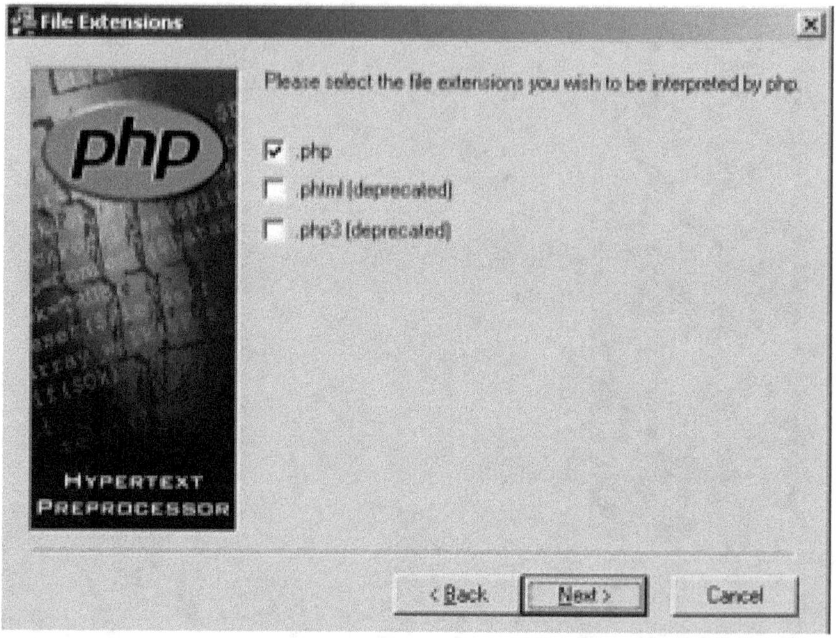

Figure 2.10: Figure 2.10 PHP Extensions

If we're lucky, we won't encounter any problems during our installation, and our Apache HTTP Server will be configured for us. However, if we receive an error message, we'll need to do some manual configurations. These will be explained in the next section. Either Apache HTTP Server is now configured, or we'll need to configure it manually. The good news is that PHP has been successfully installed (see Figure 2.11).

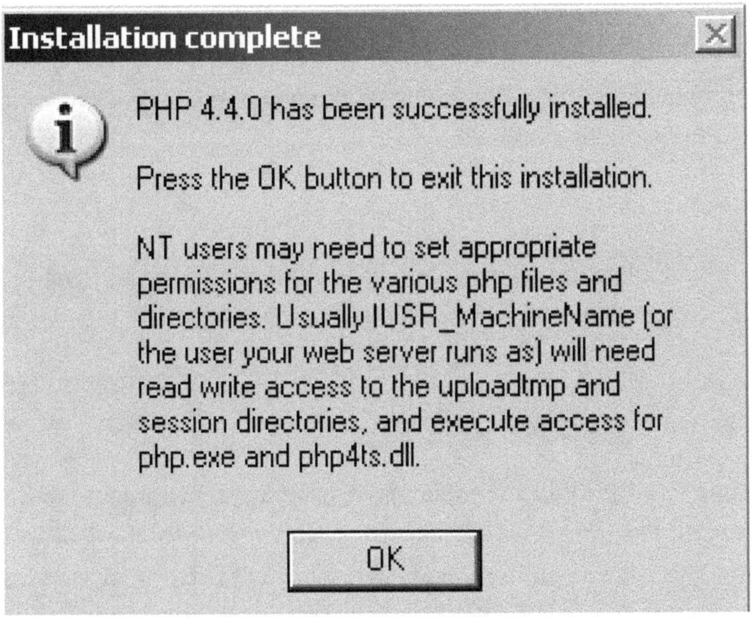

Figure 2.11: PHP Successfully Installed

Manual Configuration of HTTP Server

If the automatic configuration did not occur, we'll have to make some changes to our *httpd.conf* file located in the *conf* subdirectory of our Apache HTTP Server.

```
PHPIniDir "C:/Program Files/Apache Group/Apache2/PHP"
```

If you installed this variable in the Windows environment, I recommend that you set the main configuration file for PHP this way.

```
ScriptAlias /php/ "C:/Program Files/Apache Group/Apache2/php/"
```

This setting enables our Apache HTTP Server to recognize the proper extension sent in the request.

AddType application/x-httpd-php .php .phtml

This setting allows for the overriding of the MIME configuration, which is defined in the *mime.types* file.

Action application/x-httpd-php "/php/php.exe"

The Action application allows you to define media types that will execute a script whenever a matching file is called.

LoadModule php4_module "C:/Program Files/Apache Group/Apache2/php/php4apache2.dll"

This setting loads PHP as a module inside of Apache. You might need to copy this *.dll* file from the *sapi* directory under *PHP* to the PHP root directory. This is a known item, however, it doesn't occur in all cases, so simply keep this in mind and double check after the installation.

Now that we have reconfigured our Apache HTTP Server, we should restart the server. If we have done everything correctly, the server should start up just as before. If you want the server to start automatically, go into the services section of your operating system and stop and then start the services. Otherwise, simply close the Apache HTTP Server command window[6] and start the apache.exe[7] located in the *bin* subdirectory of your installation. If you only see a DOS console window, then you have successfully started the server (see Figure 2.12).

Figure 2.12: Apache HTTP Server Started

If you're reluctant to just click on the executable file to start the server, you can test your configuration script beforehand from the command prompt. Simply go to your *bin* subdirectory and load the command apache -t. This will check the syntax of the configuration file. On executing the –t option, you will either receive a message stating everything is OK or indicating where in the configuration file the error occurs (see Figure 2.13).

Figure 2.13: Syntax Check of Configuration File OK

If you would like to see all of the available command line options, change the "-t" to a "-?", and you'll get a complete list (see Figure 2.14). The ? option should work in the Linux environment as well.

Figure 2.14: Complete List of Command Line Options for the Apache HTTP Server

Now that our Apache HTTP Server is restarted and working reasonably well, let's stop it again as we need to edit our *php.ini* file located in the *PHP* subdirectory. If the file does not exist, then most likely you have installed it on a Windows operating system in which case the file is located under *C:\WINDOWS* or *C:\WINNT*. You can safely move this file to your *PHP* subdirectory. Remember, we have set the configuration file to be located inside of our *PHP* directory in the *httpd.conf* file. Now that you have the file, do a search for "doc_root" and ensure that this value is set to the same value as the "DocumentRoot" in your Apache HTTP Server *httpd.conf* file. In my case, this will be "C:/Program Files/Apache Group/Apache2/-htdocs".

Next, we need to do a bit of housework in the standard installation. In your *php.ini* file, search for "register_globals" and set it to "On" instead of "Off." Then, find the "extension_dir" and be sure to set it to "C:\Program Files\Apache Group\Apache2\PHP\ext\", or "C:\Program Files\Apache Group\Apache2\PHP\extensions" depending on the setup of your PHP directory structure (see Figure 2.15).

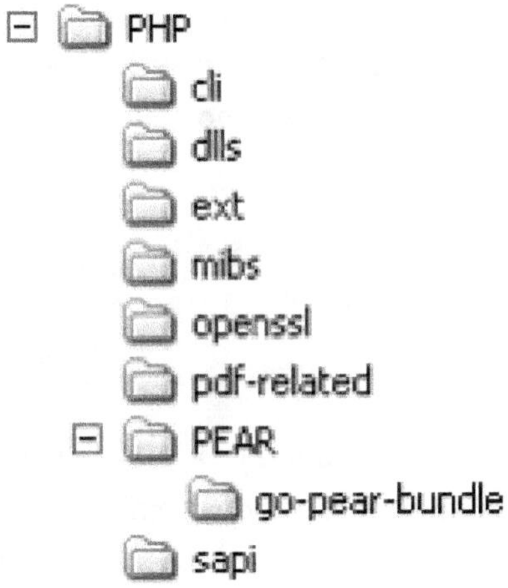

Figure 2.15: PHP Directory Listing under Apache2

The final setting in our *httpd.conf* file will be to enable our forthcoming *index.php* to load without typing "index.php". Open your *httpd.conf* and do a search for "DirectoryIndex". This parameter defines the files that will load automatically when a URL is given such as *http://localhost:8080/su01/*. By default, the line looks similar to this:

DirectoryIndex index.html index.html.var

We need to modify it to look as follows:

DirectoryIndex index.php index.html index.html.var

Next, we should be able to load a very simple PHP page within our browser.

The First PHP webpage

At this point, we have a working HTTP Server as well as an integrated

PHP. Now it's time to make our first sample page.[8] The classic "Hello World" is the one we will try as our first example.

This is the simplest of examples that one can choose (see Listing 2.2), but I think it's a good foundation to build upon as we move into areas of greater complexity.

```
<?php  echo 'Hello World';?>
```

Listing 2.2 PHP Code for Hello World Example

The echo command in PHP is similar to the System.out.println in Java or the WRITE: command in ABAP. PHP code is contained within the <?php and the ending ?> on a page, and, similar to Java and ABAP (albeit a period instead of a semicolon is used), each line ends with a semicolon.

Figure 2.16: Command Line Execution of File

When executing this simple code, you have two choices: save the file to your *htdocs* directory and execute it from your browser, or execute it from the command line using php –f helloworld.php (see Figure 2.18). Ensure that you have added the location of your *php.exe* file to your system path statement before you attempt to execute the code from the command line.

If you executed this file in your browser (see Figure 2.17), look at the current state of the file's source code. You may be surprised to see that all of the PHP coding is gone and only the words "Hello World" (see Figure 2.18) remain.

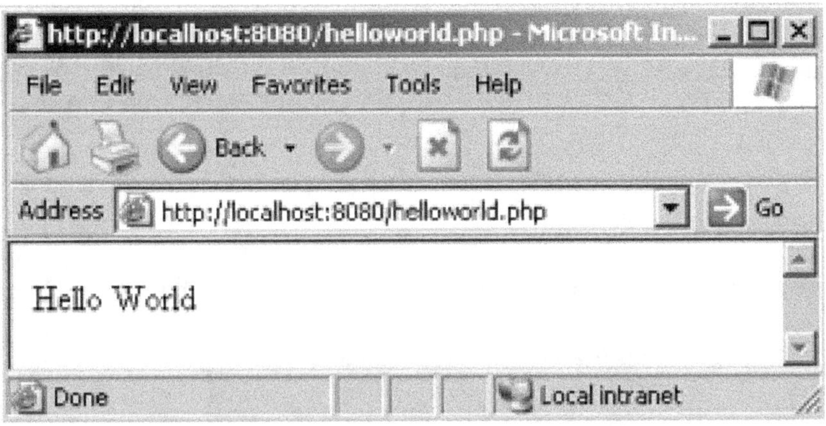

Figure 2.17: Browser Executed Version of File

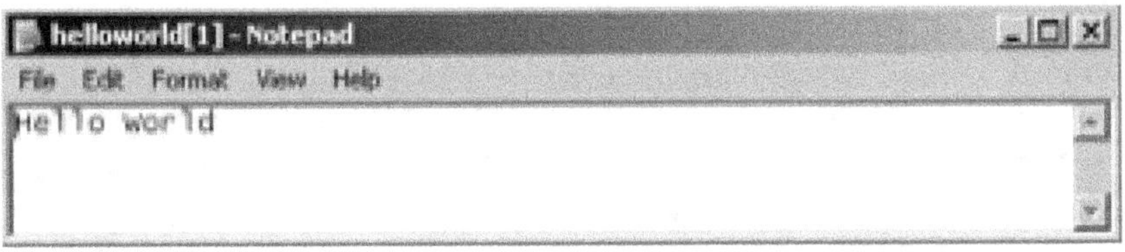

Figure 2.18: Source Code of Compiled Example

With those changes now in place, and having successfully executed our example, we are now ready to install SAPRFC and move into examples that deal more specifically with the SAP system.

SAPRFC

You can download the latest version of SAPRFC, or, at least the version that functions with your current setup.

http://saprfc.sourceforge.net

https://github.com/piersharding/php-sapnwrfc

Unpack the file directly under your *htdocs* subdirectory. Once the file is there, you will need to do some minor configuration changes to your *php.ini* file:

Ensure that this directory is pointing properly to your extension directory under PHP:

extension_dir = "C:\Program Files\Apache Group\Apache2\PHP\ext\"

Next, add the *saprfc.dll* to the extension list:

extension=php_saprfc.dll

Copy the *php_saprfc.dll* to the extension directory from where you unpacked the SAPRFC package.

With those items in place and a restart of the Apache HTTP Server, SAPRFC should be installed and ready to use (see Figure 2.19).

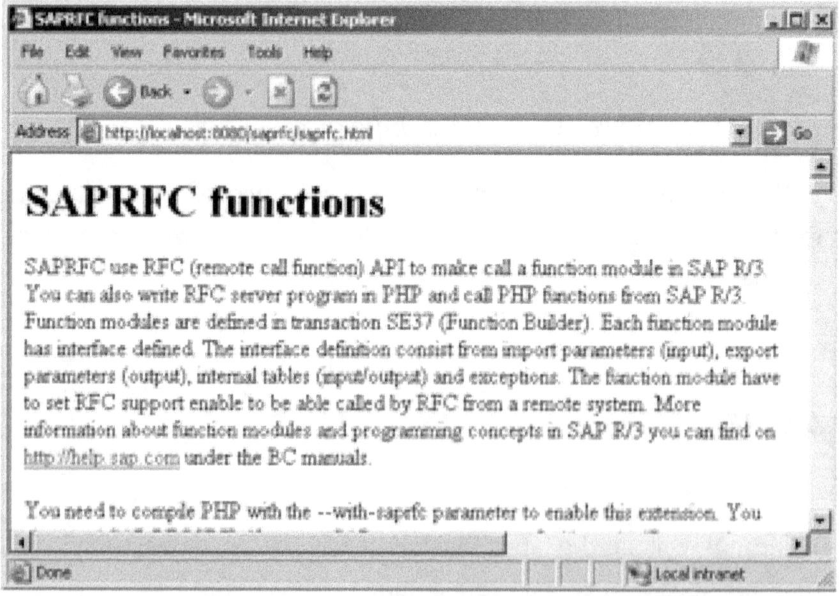

Figure 2.19: SAPRFC Start and Information Page

Now do one final check to verify that SAPRFC loads as expected, and load the *saprfc_test.php* file from your *saprfc* directory (http://localhost:8080/saprfc/saprfc_test.php). If this file loads with errors (see Figure 2.20), you'll need to revisit your error_reporting setting in your *php.ini* file and set it to:

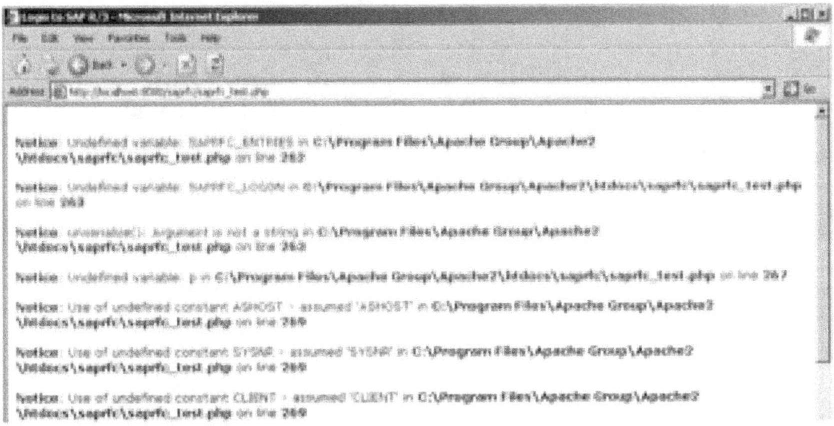

Figure 2.20: error_reporting = E_ALL & ~E_NOTICE

By changing the setting, and restarting your Apache HTTP Server and reloading the page, you should see the same results as shown in Figure 2.21.

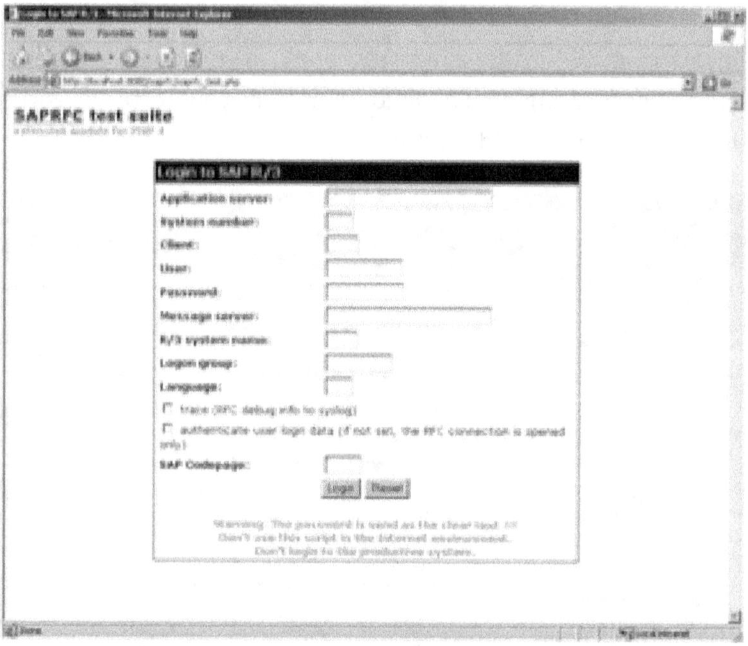

Figure 2.21: Proper Execution of SAPRFC_TEST Page

Connecting PHP to SAP

At this point, our development environment is almost complete. The only remaining task is to install the SAP GUI, unless you have already installed the Java Connector (JCo) or one of the other connectors. The RFCSDK[1] will also suffice; each of these items is available from *http://service.sap.com*.

With one of the above items installed on your system you will now have the necessary DLL's in place, we should be able to connect to a SAP system and log in. I will use the example from SAPRFC to retrieve a user list from the system (see Listing 3.1).

```
<html>

<body>

<h1>SAPRFC class: Get list of users in SAP
system</h1>

<? // Example for using the SAPRFC class library for
accessing SAP functions via RFC

// provided by Lars Laegner, btexx business
technologies, August 2001

// !!!! PLEASE CHANGE THE LOGIN DATA TO YOUR SAP
SYSTEM !!!!

// $Id: example_userlist.php,v 1.2 2001/08/16
15:54:35 llaegner Exp $

// SAPRFC class library

require_once("saprfc.php");

// Create SAPRFC instance

$sap = new saprfc(array(

"logindata"=>array(

"ASHOST"=>"2.2.2.183" // application server

,"SYSNR"=>"00" // system number
```

```
,"CLIENT"=>"000" // client

,"USER"=>"cmehcr1" // user

,"PASSWD"=>"xxxxxxx" // password

)

,"show_errors"=>false // let class printout errors

,"debug"=>false)) ; // detailed debugging information

// Call function

$result=$sap->callFunction("SO_USER_LIST_READ",

array( array("IMPORT","USER_GENERIC_NAME","*"),

array("TABLE","USER_DISPLAY_TAB",array())

));

// Call successful?

if ($sap->getStatus() == SAPRFC_OK) {

// Yes, print out the user list

?><table>

<tr><td>SAP name</td><td>User number</td></tr><?

foreach ($result["USER_DISPLAY_TAB"] as $user) {

echo "<tr><td>",
$user["SAPNAM"],"</td><td>",$user["USRNO"],¬

"</td></tr>";

}

?></table><?

} else {

// No, print long version of last error

$sap->printStatus();

// or print your own error message with the strings
```

```
received from
// $sap->getStatusText() or $sap->getStatusTextLong()
}
// Logoff/Close SAPRFC connection LL/2001-08
$sap->logoff();
?>
</body>
</html>
```

Listing 3.1: Example User List to Connect to SAP Using SAPRFC

The coding may look complicated. Let's take the code apart piece by piece and see what's happening.

Using the Classes

SAPRFC comes with several tools and packages that are already defined and, as any good developer knows, there is no point in reinventing the wheel. So, to take full advantage of these tools, we will simply "use" the defined class (see Listing 3.2).

```
// SAPRFC class libraryrequire_once("saprfc.php");
```

Listing 3.2: SAPRFC Class Library

By doing this, we now have the full functionality of the SAPRFC class available inside of our page.

Making the Connection

With the class now available, it's easy to make our connection to our SAP system. I will be making a connection to the local Mini Web AS 6.20 system that I have installed. This will help to accelerate development, unless you need to work with a specific module or component.

```
// Create SAPRFC instance$sap = new saprfc(array(
"logindata"=>array(
"ASHOST"=>"2.2.2.183"

,"SYSNR"=>"00"

,"CLIENT"=>"000"

,"USER"=>"cmehcr1"
,"PASSWD"=>"xxxxxxx"                    )
,"show_errors"=>false
,"debug"=>false)) ;
```

Listing 3.3: SAPRFC Instance, Connection to a System

As you can see in Listing 3.3, we are defining the following information (see Table 3.1) to make the connection.

Parameter	Value
ASHOST	IP or Host name of your server
SYSNR	System number of your instance
CLIENT	Login client
USER	User name

PASSWD	Password

Table 3.1 Parameter Listing for Creating a SAPRFC Instance

Calling the Function

Once a connection is made to the system, you just need to decide on which ABAP function to call in order to retrieve the data or submit the data that you want. In this example, we're calling a standard ABAP function SO_USER_LIST_READ, which you can log into your system and review, and see in detail under Transaction SE37 (see Figure 3.1).

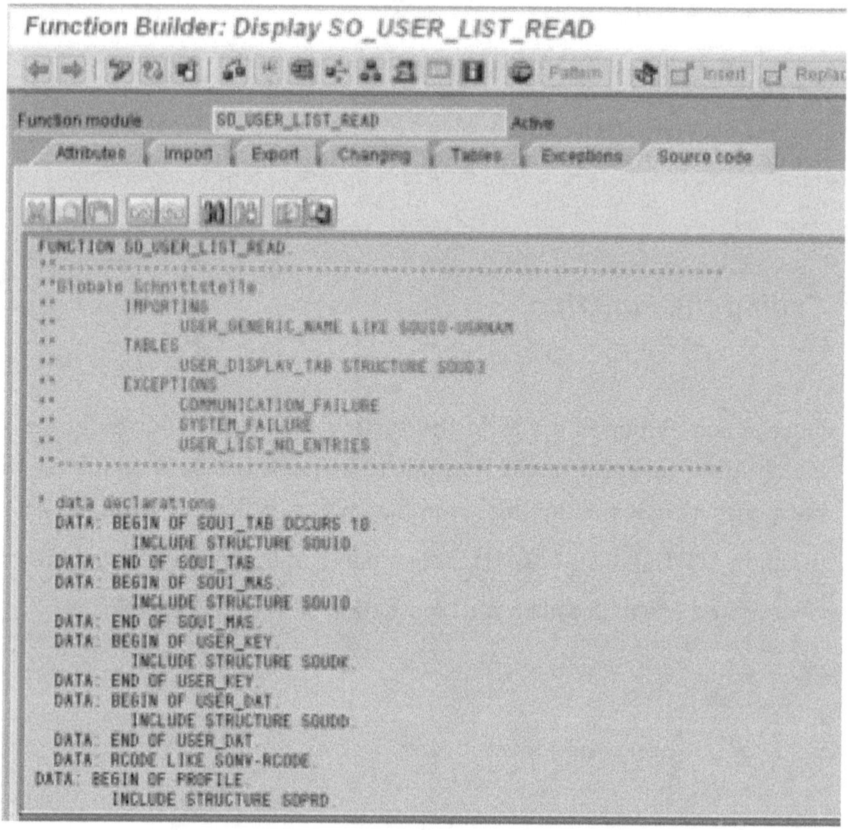

Figure 3.1: Details of SO_USER_LIST_READ in Transaction SE37

Most important is to check the **Attributes** tab (see Figure 3.2) and ensure that the function module is a **Remote-enabled module**; otherwise, we will not be able to call it using PHP or any other external programming language.

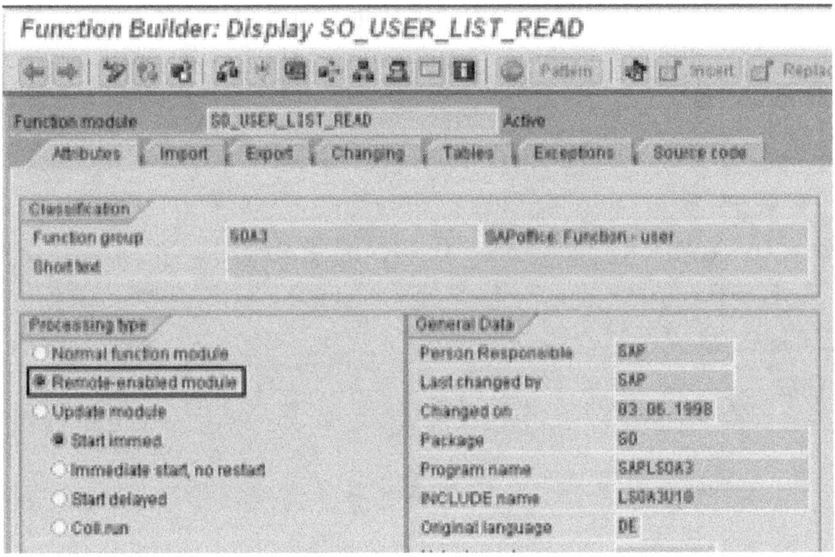

Figure 3.2: Ensure That the Function Module Is Remote-Enabled

It's relatively easy to make the call. Simply define the name and the IMPORT and EXPORT parameters or, in our case, the TABLES parameters (see Listing 3.4).

```
// Call function

$result=$sap->callFunction("SO_USER_LIST_READ",

array(array("IMPORT","USER_GENERIC_NAME","*"),

array("TABLE","USER_DISPLAY_TAB",array())

));
```

Listing 3.4: Calling a Function Using SAPRFC Methods

To find these items of information, simply review the following tabs in SE37, **Import**, **Export**, and **Tables** (see Figure 3.3 and Figure 3.4). The import parameters of the function module are showing that USER_GENERIC_NAME is a required parameter. The tables parameters of the function module are showing the name of the table and the structure of the table—SAPRFC will handle the structure types automatically. We don't have to change anything regarding the export parameters.

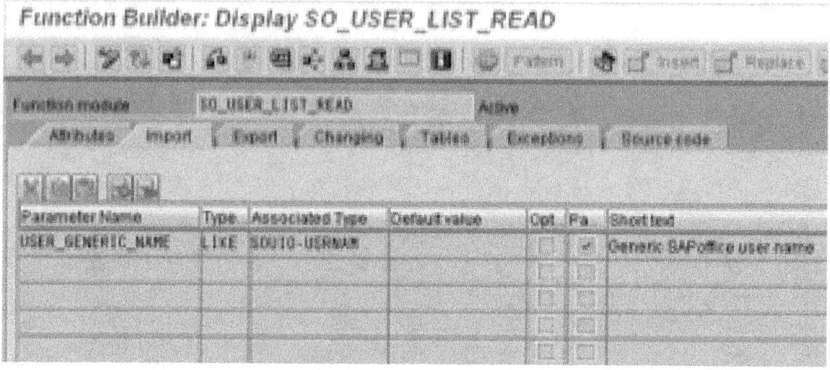

Figure 3.3: Import Parameters

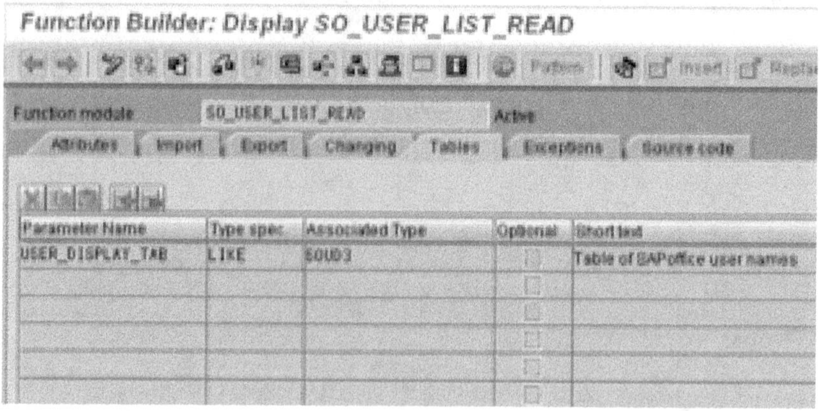

Figure 3.4: Tables Parameters

Reading the Result

Now that the connection has been made and the function has been called, it's always wise to verify whether the result is OK, which is akin to checking IF SY-SUBRC EQ 0. in ABAP (see Listing 3.5).

```
// Call successful?if ($sap->getStatus() ==
SAPRFC_OK) {

// Yes, print out the user list} else {

// No, print long version of last

// error        $sap->printStatus();

// or print your own

// error message with the

// strings received from

// $sap->getStatusText() or

// $sap->getStatusTextLong()}
```

Listing 3.5: IF Statement to Determine Whether the Result of the Function Call Is OK

If our result is not OK, we will output the status that shows the system error messages. If the result is OK, we will then need to loop through the result—in this case, the export parameter was a table—and then display the results on the page (see Listing 3.6).

```
// Call successful?

if ($sap->getStatus() == SAPRFC_OK) {

// Yes, print out the user list

?><table>

<tr><td>SAP name</td><td>User number</td></tr><?

foreach ($result["USER_DISPLAY_TAB"] as $user) {
```

```
echo "<tr><td>",
$user["SAPNAM"],"</td><td>",$user["USRNO"],"</td></tr
>";

}

?></table><?

} else {

// No, print long version of last error

$sap->printStatus();

// or print your own error message with the strings
received from

// $sap->getStatusText() or $sap->getStatusTextLong()

}
```

Listing 3.6: HTML and PHP Coding to Display the Results of the Table

The results include each user in the client that we have logged into (see Figure 3.5).

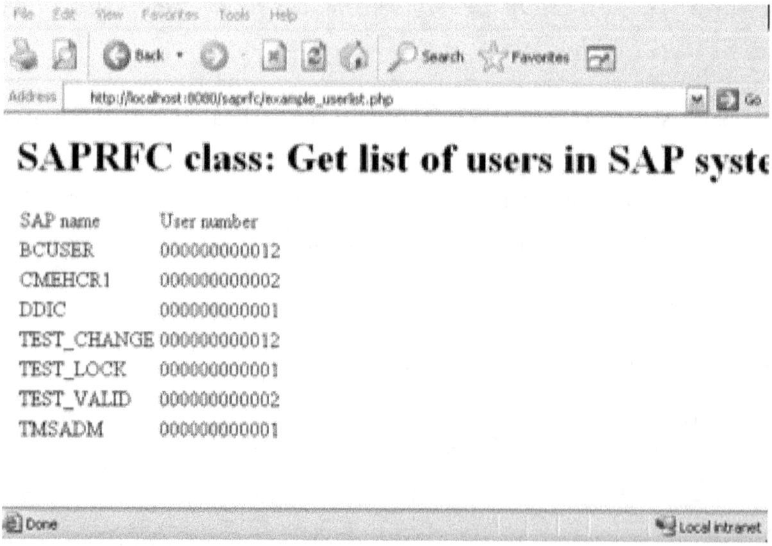

Figure 3.5: User List

Logging Off

Lastly, we come to logging off. This is one of those small but very important steps that we need to do. After we have logged off (see Listing 3.7) and everything is working properly, it is time to move onto our example application, which I will lay out and describe for you as we move along.

```
// Logoff/Close SAPRFC connection

// LL/2001-08

$sap->logoff();
```

Listing 3.7: Logging Off from SAPRFC Connection

Example Application

With most programming languages, it is better to have a solid workable example to learn from, and, since I will be using the Mini Web AS 6.20 system and I want to ensure that the example provided will work on virtually any SAP system, I will use an example that deals with user information within the SAP system. Generally, this example will serve as a smaller alternative to some of the functionalities available with Transaction SU01 (see Figure 4.1).

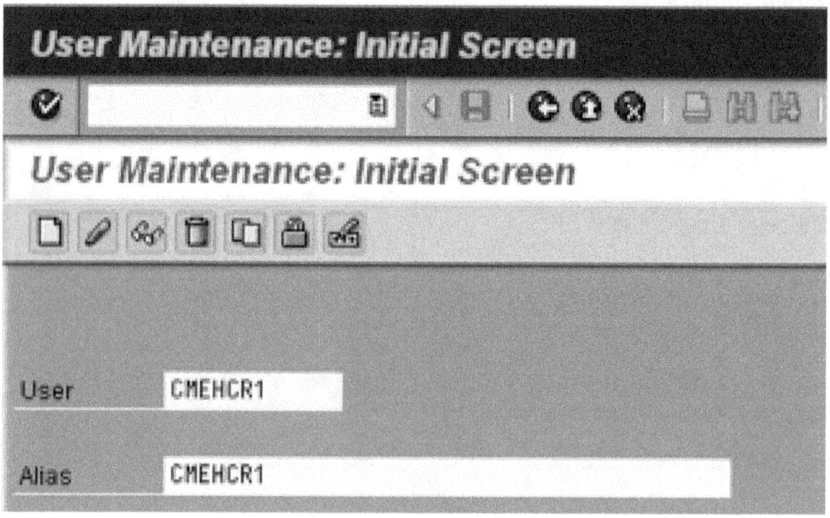

Figure 4.1: Standard SU01 Transaction

The Problem

Our task will be to basically recreate some of the standard functionalities of SU01 within a PHP-based website. The idea is to work with the following items (see Figure 4.2):

Lock User

Unlock User

User List

User Information

User Validity

Each of these items will be used in a website design using PHP and with direct interaction to the SAP system.

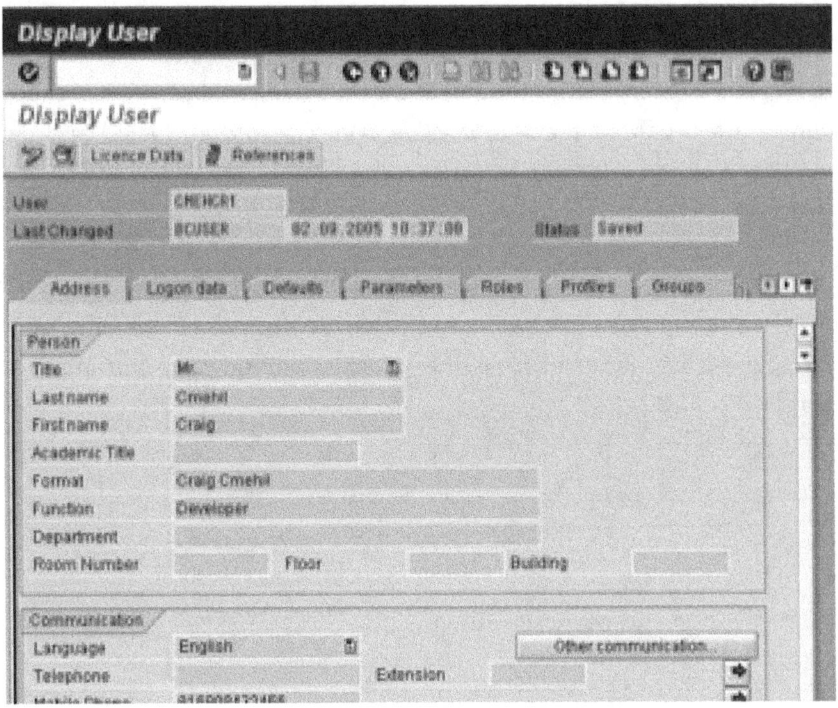

Figure 4.2: User Details in SU01

We won't cover each of these items in Transaction SU01 in detail, but you will get an idea of how to work with PHP and SAP, which is the primary goal of our example application, plus you'll learn about some basic HTML items, JavaScript,[1] and a little CSS[2] and DHTML.[3]

With any application—particularly one that is web-based—it is always best to start by laying out your page. You have a limited area in which to work; therefore, it's to your advantage to see how you can best fit your application layout, functions, and output without making your page too large or too crowded. One of the main things to do when creating a web-based application is to determine what sort of "display environment" you have to work with, that is, the size of the browser window, the resolution, the type of browser, and so forth. If this website is intended for the general Internet audience, then you should consult the various websites containing statistics and information about what the popular browser of choice is at the moment and the various pieces of data that go along with that. Some of the most popular web developers' sites that you should check out are those at W3Schools, which are a part of the *World Wide Web Consortium* (W3C) and deal with the standards and Internet, specifically the *World Wide Web* (WWW).

Knowing which browser the bulk of the population uses (see Figure 4.3) will help as you move forward with coding as there are still differences in how each browser displays the information you have put into your page.

2005	IE 6	IE 5	Ffox	Moz	NN 7	O 8	O 7
August	68.4%	6.3%	18.9%	2.4%	0.4%	0.8%	0.3%
July	67.9%	5.9%	19.8%	2.6%	0.5%	0.8%	0.4%
June	65.0%	6.8%	20.7%	2.9%	0.6%	0.7%	0.5%
May	64.8%	6.8%	21.0%	3.1%	0.7%	0.7%	0.6%
April	63.5%	7.9%	20.9%	3.1%	0.9%	0.4%	1.0%
March	63.6%	8.9%	18.9%	3.3%	1.0%	0.3%	1.6%
February	63.9%	9.5%	17.9%	3.3%	1.0%		1.7%
January	64.8%	9.7%	16.6%	3.4%	1.1%		1.9%
2004	**IE 6**	**IE 5**	**Moz**	**NN3**	**NN 7**	**NN 4**	**O 7**
December	65.5%	9.9%	17.0%	0.2%	1.2%	0.2%	1.8%
November	66.0%	10.2%	16.5%	0.2%	1.2%	0.3%	1.6%
October	67.3%	10.8%	14.7%	0.3%	1.3%	0.3%	1.6%
September	67.8%	11.2%	13.7%	0.3%	1.4%	0.3%	1.7%
August	67.0%	13.0%	12.7%	0.4%	1.4%	0.4%	1.6%
July	67.2%	13.2%	12.6%	0.4%	1.4%	0.4%	1.6%
June	67.6%	13.2%	12.2%	0.5%	1.4%	0.4%	1.6%
May	68.1%	13.8%	9.5%	0.6%	1.4%	0.4%	1.6%
April	68.2%	14.0%	8.5%	0.8%	1.4%	0.6%	1.4%
March	68.2%	14.6%	7.9%	0.8%	1.4%	0.6%	1.4%
February	68.3%	15.2%	7.3%	0.6%	1.5%	0.4%	1.5%
January	68.9%	15.8%	5.5%	0.4%	1.5%	0.5%	1.5%

Figure 4.3: W3Schools Statistics on Browser Usage Month by Month

Some of you will either consider yourselves lucky or perhaps not so lucky if you're stuck with a particular browser, which most of are in the "browser politics" of our companies. In many cases, your company/client has a standard browser and settings they use within their organization, which will be considered standard in many cases. This will make things much easier for you, because you don't have to cater to various "cross browser" issues with a rendering of HTML elements and CSS elements. If you're not sure of what your company/client standards are, you should ask for a copy of their application and style guides, which usually contain these standards.

The display resolution is a trend that most of us dealing with web development follow very closely since we all want a larger area to work with. Even though the statistics (see Figure 4.4) show that over 55% of the people in July of 2005 are using 1024 × 768, it's still safer to work in 800 × 600. But, for the purpose of this book and our example, we'll take advantage of these numbers and use 1024 × 768, simply because we can. However, please keep these numbers and this warning in mind as you move forward after our example.

2005	Higher	1024x768	800x600	640x480	Unknown
July	14%	55%	25%	0%	6%
January	12%	53%	30%	0%	5%
2004	**Higher**	**1024x768**	**800x600**	**640x480**	**Unknown**
July	10%	50%	35%	1%	4%
January	10%	47%	37%	1%	5%
2003					
July	8%	43%	44%	2%	5%
January	6%	40%	47%	2%	5%
2002					
October	6%	38%	49%	2%	5%

Web developers be aware: Many users still have only 800x600 display screens.

Figure 4.4: Display Resolution Statistics from W3School

Another important item to consider is whether a browser can run JavaScript (see Figure 4.5). Often, JavaScript is used to create dynamic effects on a page.

2005	JavaScript On	JavaScript Off
July	90%	10%
January	89%	11%
2004	**JavaScript On**	**JavaScript Off**
July	90%	10%
January	92%	8%
2003		
July	89%	11%
January	89%	11%
2002		
October	88%	12%

Figure 4.5: W3Schools Statistics on JavaScript Usage

However, statistics can be misleading, and it is a matter of the group and the questions asked in any survey, how the results turn out. In all cases, you should know who your specific audience is and what their needs are (i.e., what they use to program), and build something to meet their needs.

Due to the numerous styles and application layouts, this can be complicated when working within the SAP environment; however, simultaneously, because of the numerous web-based applications that SAP now has available, most styles are readily on hand and it's simply a matter of following the guidelines in place.

Now, with a head full of numbers from looking at all these statistics, let's build our application layout. We know that we have a few items to accomplish such as knowing who is working on the page, and the time and date of who is working on what. Therefore, we should also have headers and a user list. The items in this list are the ones that we want to work with (similar to a navigation menu). Lastly, we should have the user details and actions that will constitute the body of our page.

In our layout (see Figure 4.6), we now have three defined areas. The user login information will be displayed in the top left and the date and actual time will be displayed in the top right. On the left side of our layout, we'll display our user list with the values of the ID, i.e., are they currently locked or unlocked and are they currently a valid user in the system. When you click on a name of a particular user in the user list, the details of that user will appear on the right side of our layout, along with actions that can be taken such as locking or unlocking the user.

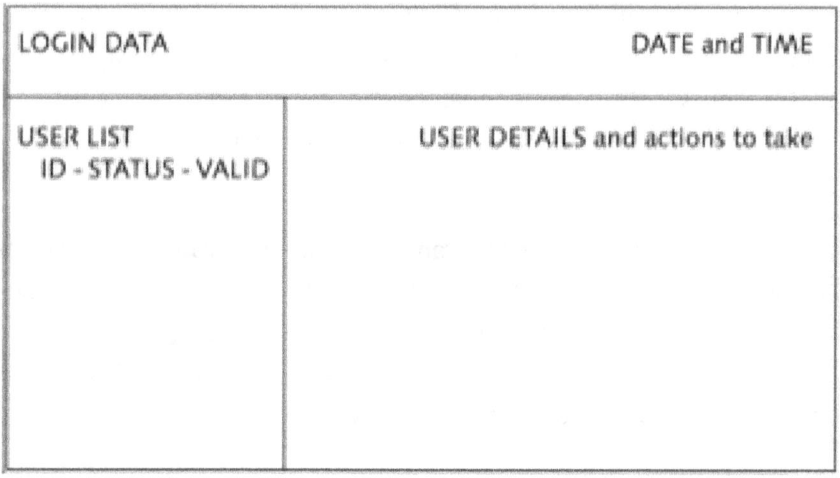

Figure 4.6: Layout of Example Application

The Background

We now a have an application layout as well as a clear idea of what we want to put into the application, but, before we start, I want to provide you with some of my reasoning behind building such an application. It is true that Transaction SU01 has all of these features and it makes little sense to reinvent the wheel, however, what happens if you have a user or set of users who need to modify only a small amount of this information and you don't have the resources to train each person in working with the SAP GUI or even deploy the SAP GUI to every machine. It is precisely in these instances that an alternative means of having the users work is usually necessary. A web-based solution is often ideal when there is a high turnaround on the equipment being used, for example, a computer in a manufacturing environment may not have the expected lifespan of one in an office environment; therefore, there needs to be a quick mechanism in place to replace PCs that no longer work and still allow the user to work again as quickly as possible.

Let's look at something more along the lines of the example we are building. We have a university or other large organization that typically uses Transaction SU01 to enter every single student or member of their organization, however, during the time period they sign up the most individuals, they're sitting in a rather large and open area with a lot of activity. Now it's critical that they get the information into the system, but, with so much activity taking place, there is a chance that the computer will be damaged.

In this scenario, the worst happens, of course, and the computer is damaged. In the past, they most likely switched to paper and pen to get the information down, or perhaps they were lucky enough to have a backup computer waiting for them. Well, with a web-based application, they would have only two requirements: a computer connected to the network and a web browser. If their computer is damaged this time around, all they need to do is to meet those two requirements and they can continue working.

The System

So, let's get started. We have our computer/server in place and working; we have a text editor of some sort ready for us to begin programming with; and, we have our login to our SAP system in order to search and find which function modules to use and what data we want to retrieve and change from the system.

All of the following function modules can be easily and quickly located in Transaction SE37 inside of your system; you can also find several other modules that you may want to experiment with at a later date by simply entering "*USER*" in SE37 and pressing **F4** to search (see Figure 4.7).

BAPI_USER_GETLIST

BAPI_USER_GET_DETAIL

BAPI_USER_UNLOCK

BAPI_USER_LOCK

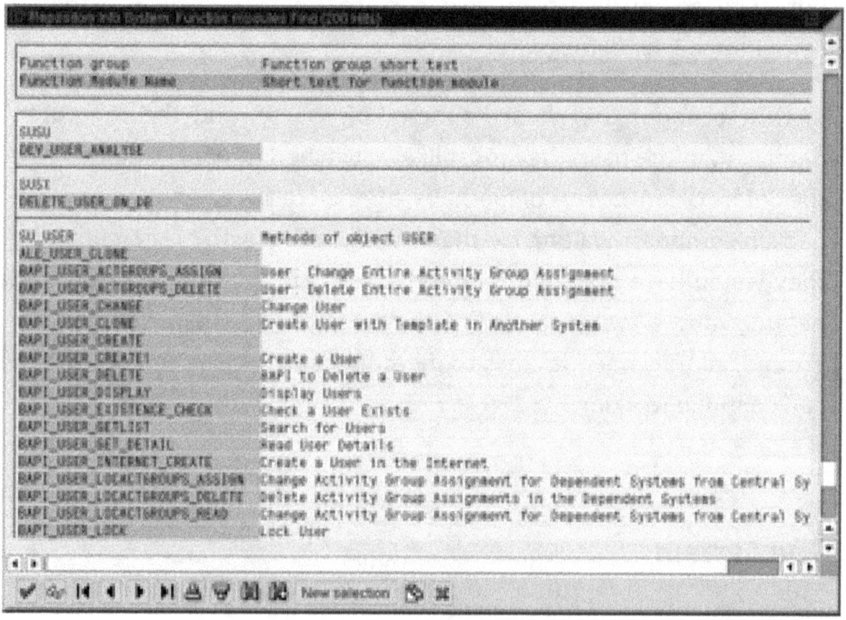

*Figure 4.7: Search in SE37 for *USER**

However, these function modules will be the main ones we'll be using.

Foundation and Connection

With most projects, we will start by building our foundation, which will consist of three parts: HTML, CSS, and PHP. This foundation will allow us to move forward with development, enabling us to add features at later dates. If we keep these Web tools in mind when creating a foundation for our project, we should have very little trouble with flexibility or scalability in the future.

Because the code is sometimes difficult to follow, especially if you aren't sure where to insert or replace the code, please see Section A.1 in the Appendix for a complete listing of the code displayed in this chapter.

HTML and JavaScript

The first layer of our foundation will be based in HTML; this will provide us with our page design and the placeholders for all of our data. The JavaScript portion of this layer will help us to create some dynamic effects, which will bring the page to life for its viewers. The steps involved are:

Create a new directory under *htdocs* called *su01*. This will be our new website.

With your editor or directly in the file system, create a new file within the *su01* directory called *index.php*. This will be the new home page of our website.

Open *index.php* inside of your editor.

Add Listing 5.1 at the beginning of the file.

```
<!DOCTYPE html PUBLIC "-//W3C//DTD XHTML 1.0
```

```
Transitional//EN"
"http://www.w3.org/TR/xhtml1/DTD/xhtml1-
transitional.dtd">

<html>

<head>

<title>SU01 Transaction</title>

<meta http-equiv="Content-Type" content="text/html;
charset=windows-1252">

<meta name="Keywords" content="SU01,user
administration,user,administration" />

<meta name="Description" content="SAP SU01
transaction support in PHP" />

<meta http-equiv="pragma" content="no-cache" />

<meta http-equiv="cache-control" content="no-cache"
/>

<link rel="stylesheet" type="text/css"
href="su01.css" />

</head>

<body>

</body>

</html>
```

Listing 5.1: Default for HTML page

Basically, we now have an HTML page that has been correctly defined, with the correct metadata in place, and a link to a CSS file. Now we can define the body content of the page, which is the area that is displayed in the browser window when the user views the page.

Insert Listing 5.2 after the <body> tag in our *index.php* page.

```
<table border="1" cellSpacing="2" cellPadding="2"
width="100%">
```

```
<tr>

<td>LOGIN INFO</td>

<td>DATE and TIME</td>

</tr><tr>

<td>USER LIST</td>

<td>USER DETAIL</td>

</tr>

</table>
```

Listing 5.2: Table to Manage the Layout of Our Page—the Placement of Data

Some developers might say that using <div> tags and pure CSS to manage the layout of the page is preferable to using placeholders for our tags and using a HTML table; however, for our purposes, this approach should suffice. With a project that is going into production, I may use <div> tags and as much CSS as possible, the reason being that as a developer I no longer need to think or worry about the way the application looks; a designer could then use CSS to completely change the layout and "look & feel" of the application.

Save the file and open your browser.

Ensure that your Apache HTTP Server is started and load the following URL: "http://localhost:8080/su01" (see Figure 5.1). Remember to change the port number to match what you have configured earlier.

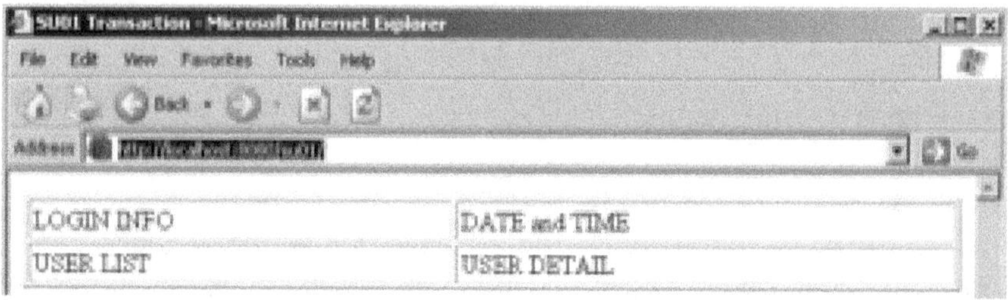

Figure 5.1: New Index Page with No Frills or Enhancements

Now that the layout is in place, we can focus on our "DATE and TIME" section. To do this, we will use a script from the website, Dynamic Drive (*http://www.dynamicdrive.com*), which is one of many websites on the Internet that is loaded with samples, examples, and code snippets for use when generating or editing web pages. By using these websites, the developer is freed up from the need to constantly rewrite code, especially since there are so many of these websites available. The use of such websites drastically accelerates development time, leaving extra time for the more complex areas of the application. Nevertheless, you should ensure that the code procured from these websites can be used in business applications.

Open the *index.php* page in your editor.

Before we add the </body> tag of the page, we need to insert Listing 5.3.

```
<script>

/*

Live Date Script - (c) Dynamic Drive
(www.dynamicdrive.com)

For full source code, installation instructions,
100's more DHTML scripts, and Terms Of

Use, visit http://www.dynamicdrive.com

*/

var dayarray=new
```

```
Array("Sunday","Monday","Tuesday","Wednesday","Thursd
ay","Friday","Saturday")

var montharray=new
Array("January","February","March","April","May","Jun
e","July","August","September","October","November","
December")

function getthedate(){

var mydate=new Date()

var year=mydate.getYear()

if (year < 1000)

year+=1900

var day=mydate.getDay()

var month=mydate.getMonth()

var daym=mydate.getDate()

if (daym<10)

daym="0"+daym

var hours=mydate.getHours()

var minutes=mydate.getMinutes()

var seconds=mydate.getSeconds()

var dn="AM"

if (hours>=12)

dn="PM"

if (hours>12){

hours=hours-12

}

if (hours==0)

hours=12
```

```
if (minutes<=9)

minutes="0"+minutes

if (seconds<=9)

seconds="0"+seconds

// Change font size here

var cdate=dayarray[day]+", "+montharray[month]+"
"+daym+", "+year+" "+hours+":"+minutes+":"+seconds+"
"+dn

if (document.all)

document.all.clock.innerHTML=cdate

else if (document.getElementById)

document.getElementById("clock").innerHTML=cdate

else

document.write(cdate)

}

if (!document.all&&!document.getElementById)

getthedate()

function goforit(){

if (document.all||document.getElementById)

setInterval("getthedate()",1000)

}

</script>
```

Listing 5.3: JavaScript Code to Display "DATE and TIME" Dynamically While the Page Is Loaded

Then, once that is in place, we need to insert <span id="clock"></span> where we have the placeholders "DATE and TIME," namely, between the <td> and </td> tags. This will be our new JavaScript placeholder for dynamically showing the date and time.

Lastly, we insert the attribute onLoad="goforit()" into the <body> tag. In the previous step, we inserted our JavaScript placeholder. Now this action calls the JavaScript method that we have inserted (see Listing 5.3), and will then dynamically generate the date and time.

CSS

For our next placeholder “replacement,” we will format our “LOGIN INFO” area to match our layout design.

Find the “LOGIN INFO” placeholder in our *index.php* file and replace it with Listing 5.4.

```
<div class="userBody">

 <span id="menu">

    <a href="index.php"><img src="images/s_B_REFR.gif"
border="0">Refresh</a>

    <img src="images/s_POSITI.gif" border="0">Ccmehil
</span>

</div>
```

Listing 5.4: User ID Coding

Save your page.

You are apt to notice that when you refresh the page, it may not meet with your aesthetic approval. With the HTML foundation in place, or at least most of it, we can now “spruce” up our page with Cascading Style Sheets (CSS). Style sheets afford us the flexibility to alter our design or modify it without having to edit the coding of the HTML itself, and therefore, Corporate Identity does not pose a problem.

You probably noticed that when we entered the items for the “LOGIN

INFO", there were some <id> tags present. These are the items that we will modify with CSS first.

Create a new file called *su01.css*. This file will contain all of our CSS formatting for the website.

Open this file with your editor and add Listing 5.5. I have used an image here called *s_POSITI.gif* and *s_B_REFR.gif* (see Listing 5.4) located in a subdirectory under *su01* called *images*, however, you can use any image that you want. Actually, all the images I will use are copies of those found within the SAP system.

Save your file and view your page.

```
.userBody {
font-size: 95%;
font-weight: bold;
background-color: white;
color: white;
border-collapse: collapse;
border: 1px solid #aaa;
padding: 0 .8em .3em .5em;
}
#menu {
font-size: 95%;
font-weight: bold;
line-height: 1.95em;
background-color: white;
color: black;
border-collapse: collapse;
```

```
border: 0px solid #aaa;

padding: 0 .8em .3em .5em;

}

#clock {

font-size: 95%;

font-weight: bold;

background-color: white;

color: black;

border-collapse: collapse;

border: 0px solid #aaa;

padding: 0 .8em .3em .5em;

}
```

Listing 5.5: Initial CSS Styles for Our Foundation

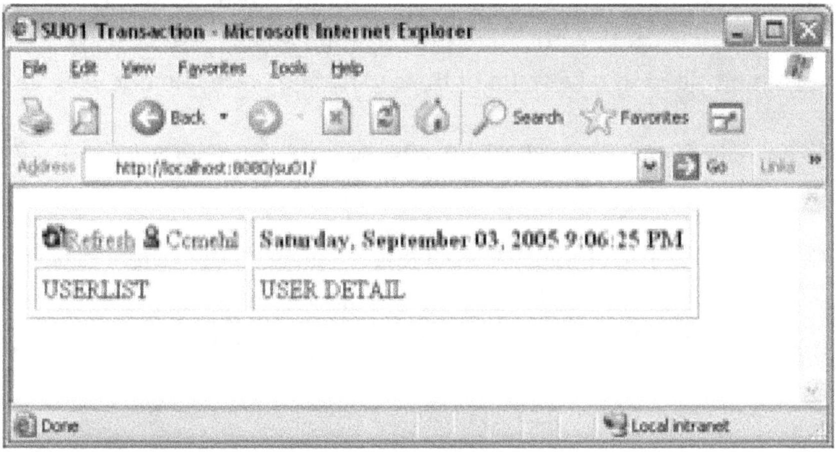

Figure 5.2: New Enhancements Using CSS

As you can see in Figure 5.2, CSS allows us to alter the appearance of elements within the page without altering the coding in the page.

There are two ways to work with CSS. The quickest way is to simply add the CSS directly into the page, however, when dealing with multiple pages, this can mean a lot of extra work for you. This brings us to the optimal way to work with CSS, and that is by using an external file. In each page of the application, you can link to the external file, thus allowing for the same "look & feel" throughout the application. The CSS file contains standard elements and custom elements and, in turn, defines each element's attributes from positioning to appearance. As a developer, this could prove very useful, especially if you need to add only the functionality but leave the design to someone else.

The rest of the information will be modified by simply adding the dynamic PHP. We'll also continue to add, alter, and adjust our HTML, JavaScript, and CSS.

PHP

We'll begin the implementation of PHP with the user list, which was the example that came with SAPRFC. We've already seen that it works, so we simply need to take some of the coding and place it in our new file.

Copy the *saprfc.php* file from the *SAPRFC* directory to our *su01* directory.

Open *index.php* and find the "USER LIST" placeholder. Then, replace it with Listing 5.6. This will show additional cell definitions and CSS style assignments and a call to a PHP function UserList($sap);.

```
<td valign="top" width="120px">

    <table>

    <tr>

    <td class="tb-header">ID</td>
```

```
    <td class="tb-header">Status</td>

    <td class="tb-header">Valid</td>

    </tr>

    <?php echo UserList($sap); ?>

    </table>

</td>
```

Listing 5.6: Replacement of the "USER LIST" placeholder

Create a new PHP file in your *su01* directory called *su01.php*, which we'll use to hold all of our functions for our page.

Open *su01.php* with your text editor and insert Listing 5.7.

```
<?php
function UserList($sap) {
// Call function
$result=$sap->callFunction("SO_USER_LIST_READ",
array( array("IMPORT","USER_GENERIC_NAME","*"),
array("TABLE","USER_DISPLAY_TAB",array())
));
// Call successful?
if ($sap->getStatus() == SAPRFC_OK) {
// Yes, print out the user list
foreach ($result["USER_DISPLAY_TAB"] as $user) {
$user_status = GetStatus($sap,$user["SAPNAM"]);
$user_valid = GetValid($sap,$user["SAPNAM"]);
```

```
$listing .= "<tr
onMouseOver=\"this.className='highlight'\"
onMouseOut=\"this.className='normal'\"><td
class=\"tb-data\">

<a
href=\"index.php?user=".$user["SAPNAM"]."\">".$user¬

["SAPNAM"]."</a></td><td class=\"tb-
data\">".$user_status."</td><td class=\"tb-
data\">".$user_valid."</td></tr>";

}

} else {

// No, print long version of last error

$sap->printStatus();

}

// Now return the list

return $listing;

}

?>
```

Listing 5.7: Function to Gather User List and Return HTML Table Rows

You should pay particular attention to the following code segment in Listing 5.7. These are standard HTML methods, which enable us to use CSS styles and create the following effect: our rows will be highlighted as we move over them with our mouse.

```
onMouseOver=\"this.className='highlight'                    \"
onMouseOut=\"this.className='normal'\"
```

Before we can retrieve a list from the system, we must first log into the system. For the purposes of this example, I made a manual login. Later, we will make this login dynamic, but for now manual will suffice. Open your *index.php* file again and insert Listing 5.8 above the <html> tag. It includes the call to SAPRFC functions, SU01 functions as well as logging into the system.

```
<?php

// SAPRFC class library and

// custom library SU01
require_once("saprfc.php");

include("su01.php");

// Now login into SAP system

$sap = login("cmehcr1","xxxxxxx");

?>
```

Listing 5.8: Header Information

Now that our page can make a call to the login function, we need to add it. Open your *su01.php* file again and insert Listing 5.9 and Listing 5.10 before the UserList($sap); function. Again, this would be a dynamic login for any system in the ideal scenario. Logoff functions are recommended with any dynamic login. For our example, closing the page will terminate the login.

```
function login($user,$pwd) {

// Create SAPRFC instance

$sap = new saprfc(array(
"logindata"=>array(
"ASHOST"=>"2.2.2.183"
,"SYSNR"=>"00"

,"CLIENT"=>"000"
```

```
,"USER"=>$user
,"PASSWD"=>$pwd                    )
,"show_errors"=>false
,"debug"=>false)) ;
return $sap;}
```

Listing 5.9: Login Function

```
function logoff($sap) {
// Logoff/Close SAPRFC connection
// LL/2001-08
$sap->logoff();}
```

Listing 5.10: Logoff Function

Before we can continue, we need to implement a few other functions that our UserList function calls. In your *su01.php* file, insert Listing 5.11 after the LogOff($sap) function. Here again, the images are from the standard SAP icons located within the system.

```
function GetStatus($sap,$uid) {
$value = "";
$input = GetStatusValue($sap,$uid);
if ($input == "UnLocked" ) {
$value = "<img src=\"images/s_S_LOOP.gif\"
border=\"0\" alt=\"".$input."\">";
```

```
} else {

$value = "<img src=\"images/s_S_LOCL.gif\"
border=\"0\"       alt=\"".$input."\">";

}

return $value;

}
```

Listing 5.11: PHP Function That Returns an HTML Image Tag

As you can see in the Listing 5.11, this PHP function calls another function. So, after this function, insert Listing 5.12. This PHP function makes a call to the system and retrieves a value, which, in this case, is retrieved from a custom ABAP function module.

```
function GetStatusValue($sap,$uid) {

$value = "";

$uid = strtoupper($uid);

$result=$sap->callFunction("Z_GET_LOCKSTATUS",
array( array("IMPORT", "USERNAME",$uid),
array("EXPORT", "STATUS",array())                  ));

  // Call successful?

if ($sap->getStatus() == SAPRFC_OK) {

// Yes, then get value

if ($result["STATUS"] == "0" ) {

$value = "UnLocked";
```

```
} else {

$value = "Locked";

}

} else {

// No, print long version of

// last error

$sap->printStatus();

}

return $value;}
```

Listing 5.12: PHP Function That Makes a Call to the System

Now, we must create our custom ABAP function module within the system. If, per chance, you know of another way to access the required data, please feel free to experiment. One way to access the required data that comes to mind, but is not released by SAP for customer use, is the ABAP function module RFC_READ_TABLE.

Log into your system and go to Transaction SE37.

Type the name of our custom function module "Z_GET_LOCKSTATUS" and choose the **Save** button (see Figure 5.3).

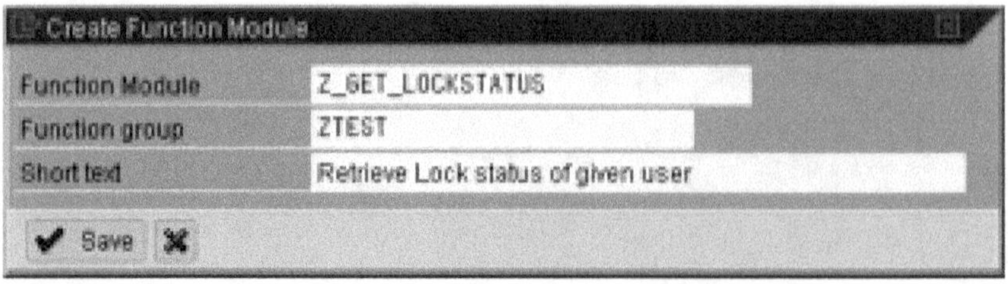

Figure 5.3: Creating Function Module in SE37

With the function module now created, we just need to set the **Remote-enabled module** attribute (see Figure 5.4) to ensure that we can use it from our PHP application.

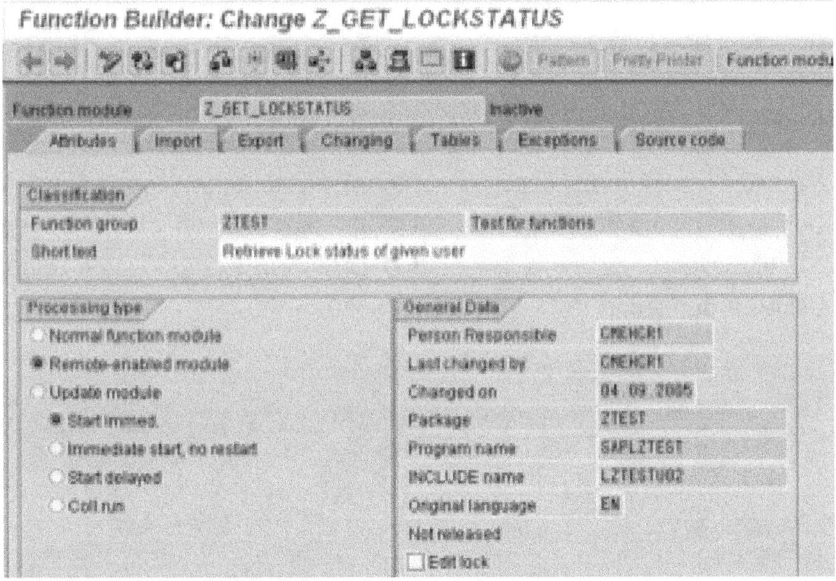

Figure 5.4: Attributes Tab

Now we need to enter the **Import** parameters for the function module (see Figure 5.5). Our import parameter will be "USERNAME" and we will define as type "USR02-BNAME" which is the field "BNAME" from the SAP table USR02. BNAME is defined as **CHAR** with a length of 12. By checking the **Pass Value**, we're saying that the parameter contents are copied when the parameter is passed and when it is transferred back. Note that this is not recommended when the parameter is a table due to the toll it takes on performance.

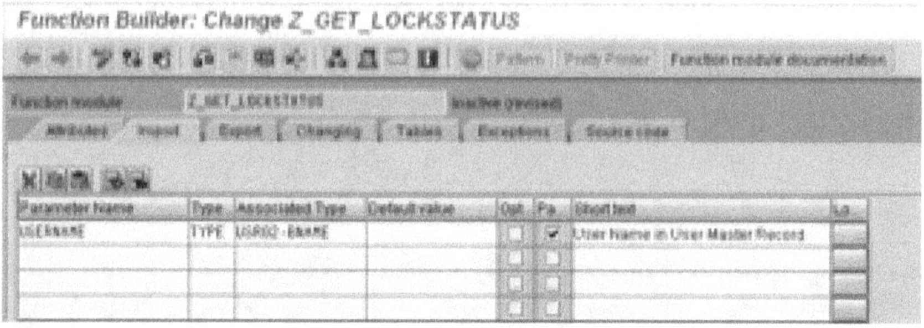

Figure 5.5: Import Tab of Our Function Module

Next, we'll set the **Export** parameters of the function (see Figure 5.6). Our export parameter will be "STATUS" and we will define as type "USR02-UFLAG," which is the field **UFLAG** from the SAP table USR02. **UFLAG** is defined as **INT1** with a length of 3.

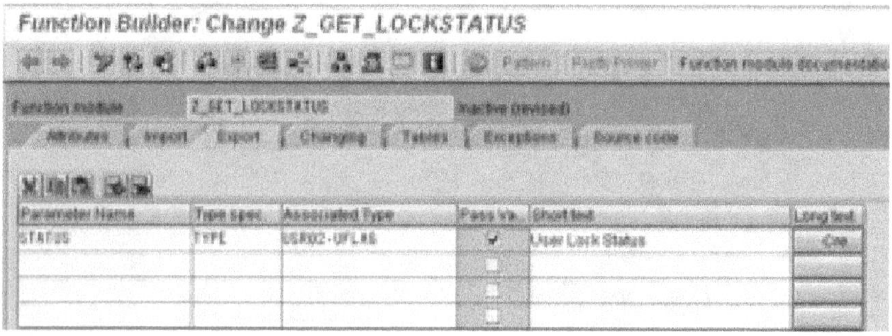

Figure 5.6: Export Tab of Our Function Module

Now switch over to the **Source Code** tab and enter Listing 5.13:

```
FUNCTION Z_GET_LOCKSTATUS.

*"----------------------------------------*"

*"Local interface:

*"  IMPORTING*"     VALUE(USERNAME) TYPE  USR02-BNAME

*"  EXPORTING*"     VALUE(STATUS) TYPE  USR02-UFLAG
```

```
*"-----------------------------------------

SELECT uflag INTO status FROM usr02  WHERE bname =
username.  ENDSELECT.ENDFUNCTION.
```

Listing 5.13: ABAP Code for Our Custom Function Module

Now you can save, check, and activate the function module. Feel free to try it out. It's very simple and direct, and should give you an idea of how easy it is to connect ABAP to PHP. You can also get an idea of how easy it would be to connect PHP to a rather complex ABAP function such as a SAP BAPI.

Once we've completed those items, we can return to our PHP page. In *su01.php*, we have entered our first few functions to get the function UserList to work. Next, we need to enter the remaining functions. Therefore, enter Listing 5.14 into the file.

```
function GetValid($sap,$uid) {

$value = "";

$result = GetUserLogonDetails($sap,$uid);

$input = $result["GLTGB"];

// Yes, then get value

if ( strtotime("now") < strtotime($input) or $input
== "00000000" ) {

$value = "<img src=\"images/s_S_OKAY.gif\"
border=\"0\" alt=\"".$input."\">";

} else {

$value = "<img src=\"images/s_S_NONO.gif\"
border=\"0\" alt=\"".$input."\">";

}

return $value;

}
```

Listing 5.14: This Function Returns Whether or Not the User Is Still Valid in the System

As you can see, this function calls GetUserLogon-Details. Therefore, we will now need to enter Listing 5.15 into our *su01.php* file. GetUserLogon-Details will return basic information about the user currently logged into the SAP system. For more information, refer to Transaction SE37 within your SAP system and the ABAP function module BAPI_USER_GET_DETAIL.

```
function GetUserLogonDetails($sap,$uid) {
$value = "";
$uid = strtoupper($uid);
$result=$sap->callFunction("BAPI_USER_GET_DETAIL",
array( array("IMPORT","USERNAME",$uid),
array("EXPORT","LOGONDATA",array())
));
// Call successful?
if ($sap->getStatus() == SAPRFC_OK) {
// Yes, then get value
$value = $result["LOGONDATA"];
} else {
// No, print long version of last error
$sap->printStatus();
}
return $value;
}
```

Listing 5.15: Function to Retrieve User Logon Data

Save the file in your editor. Then load your page in your browser as you have done previously and see if your list appears.

At this point, we should have a well-formatted list that appears when we open the page (see Figure 5.7).

If not, you should review the code changes again to ensure that nothing was missed. If the list still doesn't show up, you will need to find the *dev_rfc.trc* file, which is most likely located in your *bin* directory of Apache HTTP Server. This file contains the developer trace of your RFC connection to SAP. If the connection to SAP is working, you'll need to log into the SAP system and check Transaction ST22 to determine whether your user has caused any runtime errors. If, at this point, you are still not further along, you'll need to contact your system administrator and ask him or her to run a trace (Transaction ST05) on your user for RFC. Together, with your system administrator, you should be able to determine the cause of the problem.

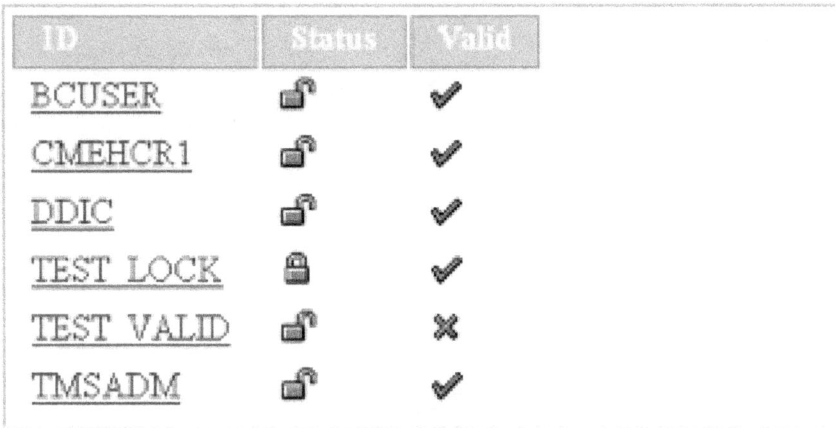

Figure 5.7: User List Outputted to the Screen with the Use of All Our PHP Coding

You'll probably notice that the list looks slightly different from yours. This is due to the CSS formatting. Therefore, we need to add the additional CSS styles now.

Open the *su01.css* file and add Listing 5.16 to complete our CSS enhancements for the list. These CSS changes will alter the apperance of the custom elements tb-header and tb-data, which have been applied to our HTML table in our page.

```
.tb-header {

font-size: 95%;

font-weight: bold;

background-color: lightgrey;

color: white;

border-collapse: collapse;

border: 1px solid #aaa;

padding: 0 .8em .3em .8em;

}

.tb-data {

align: center;

border: 0px solid #aaa;

padding: 0 .8em .3em .5em;

}
```

Listing 5.16: CSS Styles for the Table Header and Data Cells

Save the file and refresh your page.

You'll see that the highlighting of the rows is not yet activated. Therefore, we have to add Listing 5.17 to *su01.css* now. By adding these

CSS changes and then moving your mouse over the table rows you'll see that the highlighting effect is now functioning properly. What we have done is simply to instruct our page to "highlight" an element when the mouse moves over that element, that is, to simply change the background color, and when the mouse moves away to change it back.

```
.initial { background-color: #DDDDDD; color:#000000 }

.normal { background-color: #FFFFFF; }

.highlight { background-color: #8888FF }
```

Listing 5.17: CSS Styles to Make the Row Highlighting Active

Save and move your mouse over the table rows (see Figure 5.8). Provided you have incorporated the CSS changes above, saved your CSS file, and reloaded your page, you should see the table rows being highlighted as you move your mouse over them.

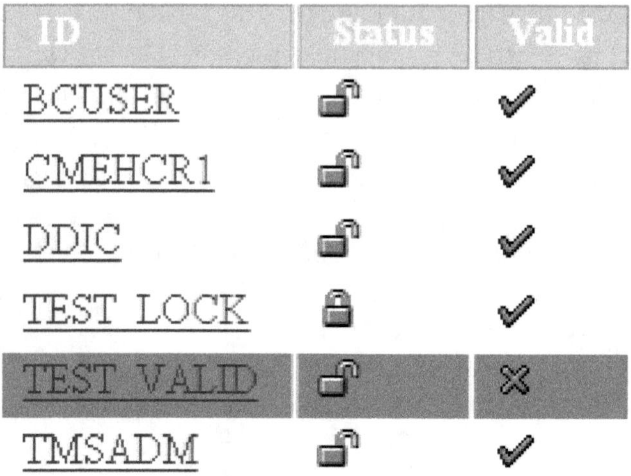

Figure 5.8: Row Highlighting Active Using CSS

Now that we have a list, what do we do with it? You've probably noticed that you can click on the name in the list. By clicking on the name, the page is sent with a parameter. We will now read that parameter and apply it to our PHP logic to load the appropriate user details in the page.

Open *index.php* and add Listing 5.18 to the top of the file, after the "login".

```
// Check if user name was clicked and

// then retrieve user details

$userid = "";

$useraddress = "";

$userlogon = "";

if (array_key_exists("user",$_GET)) {
```

```
$userid = $_GET["user"];

$useraddress = GetUserAddressDetails($sap,$userid);
$userlogon = GetUserLogonDetails($sap,$userid);

}
```

Listing 5.18: Reading User URL parameter

This gathers the parameter value of the request. In laymen's terms, GET means that you can see the parameter in the URL; POST means that the parameter values aren't visible in the URL. If you want to keep it simple and quick, using these parameters are easy and efficient. But, for more complicated scenarios or to ensure better security, sessions and cookies are preferable.

Save and click on one of the names. We can now add in the functionality for that "click," provided that your page still loads OK.

As you can see in Listing 5.18, we call the function GetUserLogonDetails, as well as a new function GetUserAddressDetails. This means that you will need to open *su01.php* and enter Listing 5.19 into the file to handle the new function call. As with GetUserLogonDetails, GetUserAddress-Details retrieves the specific address details of the user currently logged into the system.

```
function GetUserAddressDetails($sap,$uid) {

$value = "";

$uid = strtoupper($uid);

$result=$sap->callFunction("BAPI_USER_GET_DETAIL",

array( array("IMPORT","USERNAME",$uid),

array("EXPORT","ADDRESS",array())

));

// Call successful?
```

```
if ($sap->getStatus() == SAPRFC_OK) {

// Yes, then get value

$value = $result["ADDRESS"];

} else {

// No, print long version of last error

$sap->printStatus();

}

return $value;;

}
```

Listing 5.19: PHP Function to Retrieve Data from the SAP System About the User

Save *su01.php* and open *index.php* as we need to enter some HTML to display the data these two function modules retrieve for us. In the *index.php* file, insert Listing 5.20 in the "USER DETAIL" placeholder section. This will show a nice well-formatted display of user information.

```
<td valign="top" width="500px">

<div class="userDetail">

<table>

<tr>

<td class="tb-header">Last Name:</td>

<td class="tb-data"><?php echo
$useraddress["LASTNAME"] ?></td>

</tr><tr>

<td class="tb-header">First Name:</td>

<td class="tb-data"><?php echo
$useraddress["FIRSTNAME"] ?></td>

</tr><tr>
```

```
<td class="tb-header">Personal Number:</td>

<td><?php echo $useraddress["PERS_NO"] ?></td>

</tr><tr>

<td class="tb-header">Department:</td>

<td class="tb-data"><?php echo
$useraddress["DEPARTMENT"] ?></td>

</tr><tr>

<td class="tb-header">Email:</td>

<td class="tb-data"><a href="mailto:<?php echo
$useraddress["E_MAIL"]?>"><?php echo
$useraddress["E_MAIL"] ?></a>

</td>

</tr><tr>

<td colspan="2"> </td>

</tr><tr>

<td class="tb-header">Valid User until:</td>

<td class="tb-data"><?php echo
substr($userlogon["GLTGB"],0,4) ?>.<?php echo
substr($userlogon["GLTGB"],4,2) ?>.<?php echo
substr($userlogon["GLTGB"],6,2) ?></td>

</tr><tr>

<td colspan="2"> </td>

</tr><tr>

<td class="tb-header">Last Login:</td>

<td class="tb-data"><?php echo
substr($userlogon["LTIME"],0,2) ?>:<?php echo
substr($userlogon["LTIME"],2,2) ?>:<?php echo
substr($userlogon["LTIME"],4,2) ?></td>

</tr>
```

```
</table>

</div>

</td>
```

Listing 5.20: Replacement of "USER DETAIL" Placeholder

Save and reload your page by clicking on it. You should see your user data displayed (see Figure 5.9).

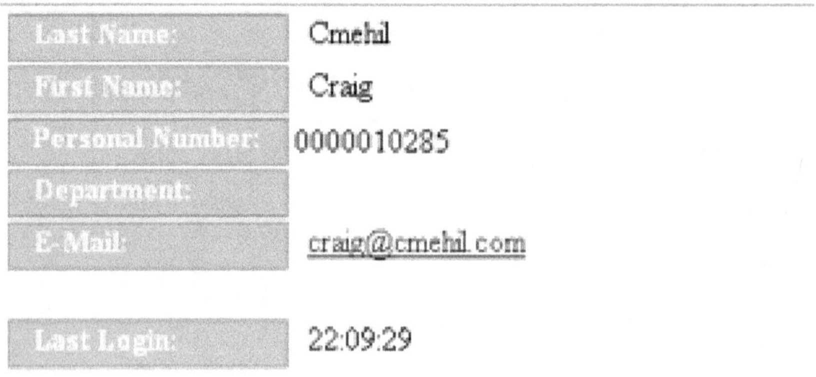

Figure 5.9: Well-Formatted Display of User Details

```
<tr>

<td colspan="2"> </td>

</tr>

<tr>

<td class="tb-header">User Action(s):</td>

<td>

<?php

if (!$userid == "" ) {

if ( GetStatusValue($sap,$userid) == "UnLocked" ) {

?>
```

```
<a href="index.php?user=<?php echo $userid
?>&action=lock"><img src="images/s_S_LOCL.gif"
border="0" alt="Lock User"></a>

<?php } else { ?>

<a href="index.php?user=<?php echo $userid
?>&action=unlock">

<?php

}

}

?>

</td>

</tr>
```

Listing 5.21: New Table Row in the "USER DETAIL" Section

Now, there's just one small item that we have to "clean up," namely, removing the border="1" in our table and replacing it with the border="0". This will remove the table border itself and leave only the resulting display of our CSS styles (see Figure 5.10).

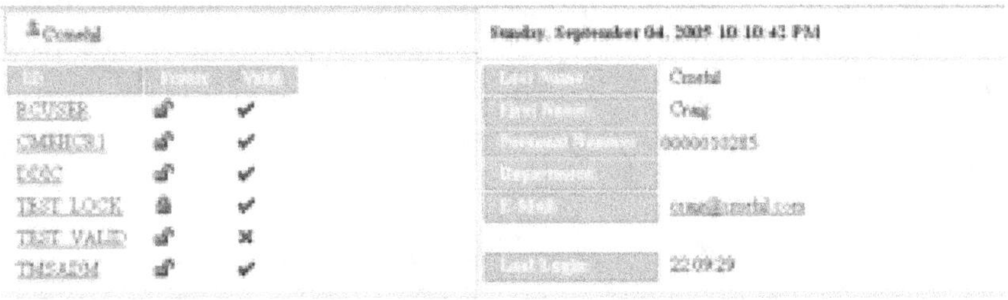

Figure 5.10: Page Showing the Table Border Set with "1"

To top off our growing application, we'll also add a refresh button and some user actions.

Open *index.php* and insert Listing 5.21 into the "USER DETAIL" section. This will add our "user action" menu into the application, allowing us to **lock** and **unlock** the user selected.

Next, we'll add Listing 5.22 to the "USER LOGIN" area before we display our "name."

```
<a href="index.php"><img src="images/s_B_REFR.gif"
border="0">Refresh</a>
```

Listing 5.22: Link That Reloads the Page

Save and reload the page (see Figure 5.11).

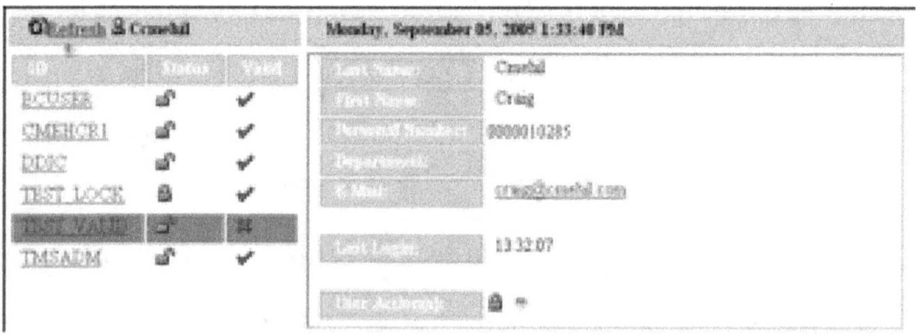

Figure 5.11: New Page Design with All New Elements in Place

Since it's helpful to have a log with most applications, we'll add an *action.log*, which will be a simple text file stored in the same directory.

Open *index.php* and append Listing 5.23 as a last row for our table.

```
</tr><tr>

<td colspan="2" class="tb-header">Action Log</td>

</tr><tr>

<td colspan="2">

<div class="userDetail">     <?php echo
ShowActionLog() ?>    </div>

</td>
```

```
</tr>
```

Listing 5.23: Two New Table Rows to Display Our "action.log"

Open su01.php and enter Listing 5.24 into the file. This will allow us to read the file. If you manually create the file called *action.log* and then add one or two lines of simple text when reloading your page, you'll see it appended to the bottom of our application.

```
function ShowActionLog() {

$filename = "action.log";

$fp = fopen($filename, "r");

$contents = fread($fp,filesize($filename));
fclose($fp);

return $contents;

}
```

Listing 5.24: Function to Display Our Log File

Save both files and reload your page. You should see your action log, in addition to the various changes to date such as the "user actions" and "user details."

Now that you have your *action.log* displayed, we need to be able to dynamically add entries to it.

Open your *su01.php* file and add Listing 5.25 to it. This will enable us to write to the file.

```
function WriteActionLog($line) {

$filename = "action.log";

$fp = fopen($filename, "a");
```

```
$string = date('l dS \of F Y h:i:s A')." -
".$line."<br>";

$write = fputs($fp, $string);

fclose($fp);

}
```

Listing 5.25: Function to Write to a File

Save your file. Of course this function only enables us to write to a file, therefore, in order to use it, we'll add in the functionality to **lock** or **unlock** a user.

Open *index.php* and add in the pieces we need to get the actions to work, find your "USER DETAIL" area, and append Listing 5.26 to the end of the file.

```
<tr><td colspan="2"> </td></tr>

<tr>

<td class="tb-header">User Action(s):</td>

<td>

<?php

if (!$userid == "" ) {

if ( GetStatusValue($sap,$userid) == "UnLocked" ) {

?>

<a href="index.php?user=<?php echo $userid
?>&action=lock"><img src="images/s_S_LOCL.gif"
border="0" alt="Lock User"></a>

<?php } else { ?>

<a href="index.php?user=<?php echo $userid
?>&action=unlock"><img src="images/s_S_LOOP.gif"
border="0" alt="UnLock User"></a>

<?php
```

```
}

}

?>

</td>

</tr>
```

Listing 5.26: Our New Action Menu

Now we have to add the coding to see whether someone has clicked on one of the action menu items. Add Listing 5.27 at the top of our *index.php* page. By adding this listing, we can capture our "action" parameter and then decide what to do with it. This listing should be inserted just before the last brace (}).

```
// Check if action was clicked$action = "";

if (array_key_exists("action",$_GET)) {

$action = $_GET["action"];

if ( $action == "lock" or $action == "unlock" ) {
ULUser($sap,$userid,$action);

}}
```

Listing 5.27: Code to Capture Action Parameter

As you can see, we have another PHP function to build. The function ULUser can help us to lock or unlock a user, thus completing the "user action" menu options. In the *su01.php* file, add Listing 5.28.

```
function ULUser($sap,$uid,$action) {

$value = "";

$uid = strtoupper($uid);

switch ($action) {
```

```
case "lock":

$result=$sap->callFunction("BAPI_USER_LOCK",

array( array("IMPORT","USERNAME",$uid),

array("TABLE","RETURN",array())

));

// Call successful?

if ($sap->getStatus() == SAPRFC_OK) {

// Yes, then get value

$value = "If allowed in the system the user, ".$uid."
has been locked";

} else {

// No, print long version of last error

$sap->printStatus();

}

break;

case "unlock":

$result=$sap->callFunction("BAPI_USER_UNLOCK",

array( array("IMPORT","USERNAME",$uid),

array("TABLE","RETURN",array())

));

// Call successful?

if ($sap->getStatus() == SAPRFC_OK) {

// Yes, then get value

$value = "If allowed in the system the user, ".$uid."
has been unlocked";

} else {
```

```
// No, print long version of last error

$sap->printStatus();

}

break;

}

WriteActionLog($value);

}
```

Listing 5.28: PHP Function to Lock or Unlock a User in the SAP System

Save the file. In Figure 5.12, you can see all of our changes to date and begin testing what you have put together.

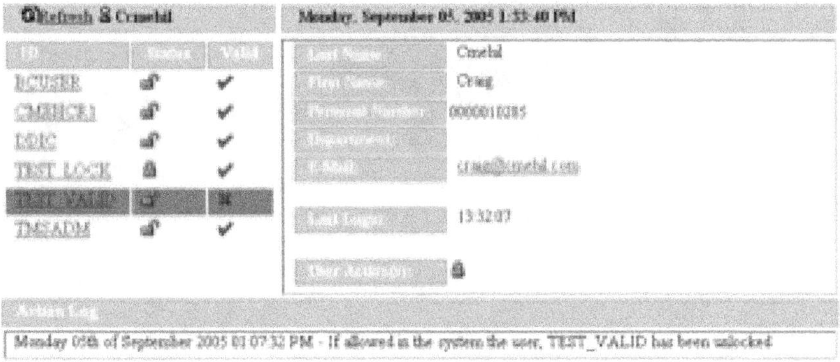

Figure 5.12: Complete Application Showing All Elements

At this point, our initial application is finished. The application should work appropriately, however, there is the possibility that when you choose to lock or unlock a user, that user is not really locked. This situation can occur when working via RFC. Therefore, you may need to implement an additional RFC call.

Open *su01.php* and insert Listing 5.29 in your ULUser function, just before we call the Write-Action-Log($value) function.

Save and try again.

```
// Now commit transaction

$result=$sap-
>callFunction("BAPI_TRANSACTION_COMMIT");
```

Listing 5.29: Committing the Transaction

Lastly, "log off" from your SAP system.

Open *index.php* and insert Listing 5.30 at the end of the page before </body> .

Save the file.

```
<?php  Logoff($sap);?>
```

Listing 5.30: Log Off From Your System

Beta Testing and Enhancements

Now that the application is ready to use and we can “lock” or “unlock” a user in our system, it’s time for us to step back, review what we did, and determine what we can do to make the application more robust.

The first area that we could improve is to create a dynamic login. Hard coding the login is of little use to anyone and it also poses a security risk, because your password is there for all to see. The second area that could stand improvement is enabling the developer to deal with the *action.log* before it becomes unwieldy. The third and last area that would improve the overall application is enabling the developer to change some of the user data.

Section A.2 (see Appendix) contains the complete listing of the final code used in this chapter. Please refer to it if you’re unsure of where to place a code segment that is given in this chapter.

Dynamic Login

To create a dynamic login, we’ll need to add a few items, for example, a login page, code to determine whether the user is logged in, and, of course a way for users to select which system they want to login to. There are two main ways of handling this: one is with cookies, and the other is to write the data to the session. Cookies are pieces of information that are stored in the browser and passed with the request. Sessions store small bits of information on the server which then exist between page calls. With a session, each instance of an application is contained in a session, and therefore, we could then have multiple users. With a cookie, the browser must accept the cookie for it to work.

Cookies

The optimal way to see this in action is via an example. It’s a very common scenario, and by doing an Internet search, you’ll likely find several examples that are very similar.

Create a new page in your *htdocs* directory called *cookie.php* and insert Listing 6.1 into this page.

Save the file and load it in your browser.

```
<?php

// Check if the request, "cookie", has the count
parameter

if(!isset($count)) {

// If not set, set it to zero

$count = 0;

// Set the cookie with the current time

$start = time();

setcookie("start", $start, time()+600, "/", "", 0);

} else {

// Otherwise increment the count

$count++;

}

// Update the cookie "count" with the current value
and time
```

Listing 6.1: Simple Cookie Example

On first load, the page will look like Figure 6.1 and with the second load, it will look like Figure 6.2. Each consecutive load after that will show an increase in the values. If, however, you look at Figure 6.3, you'll see that by adding a second browser instance, the page loaded starts with the same cookie information. This is because a cookie is stored in the browser or browser temporary cache, so if two instances of the browser are loaded, the cookie reflects the same information. If you were to load a second browser on your machine with a different temporary cache location, you would see that the cookie is different (see Figure 6.4).

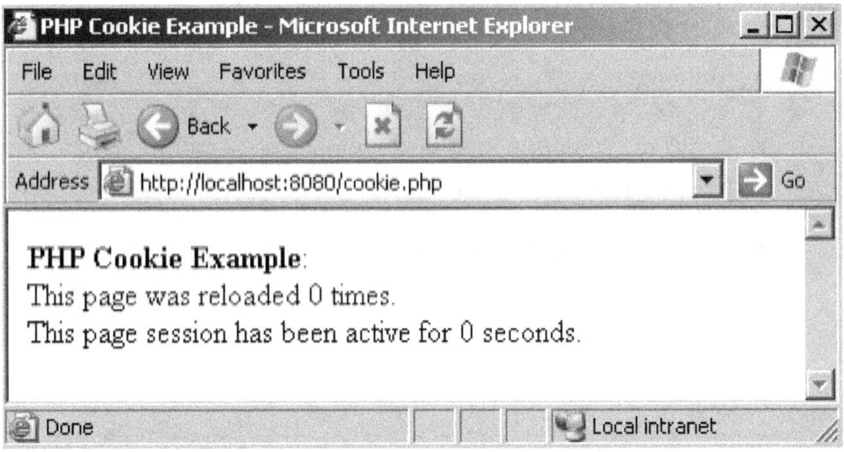

Figure 6.1: First Load of Cookie Example

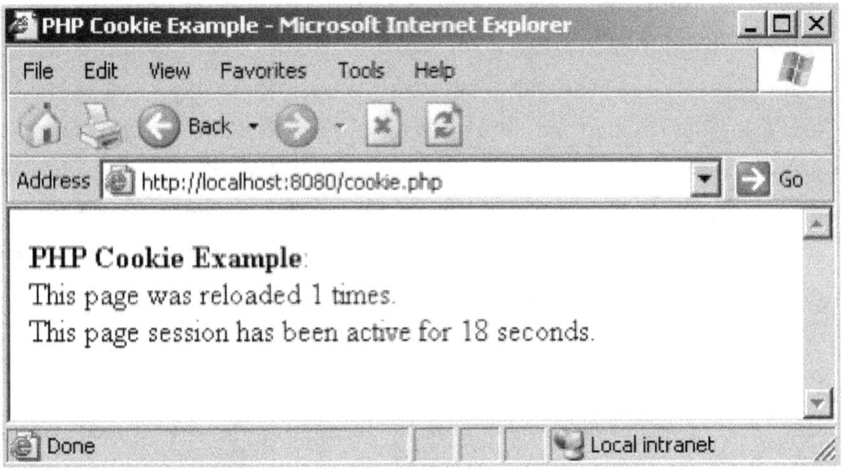

Figure 6.2: Second Load of Cookie Example

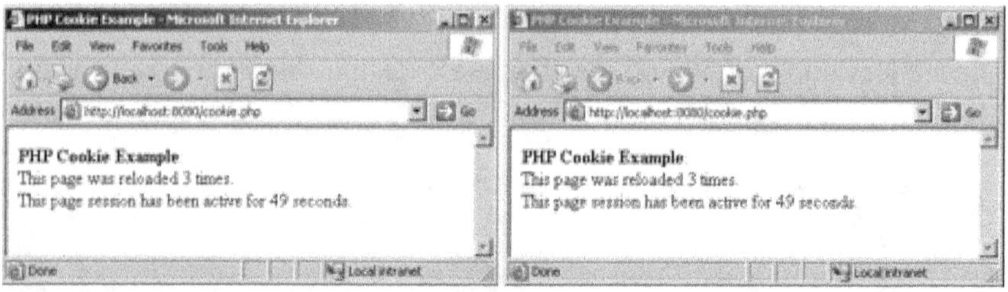

Figure 6.3: Two Instances of the Browser Showing the Same Information as Retrieved from the Cookie

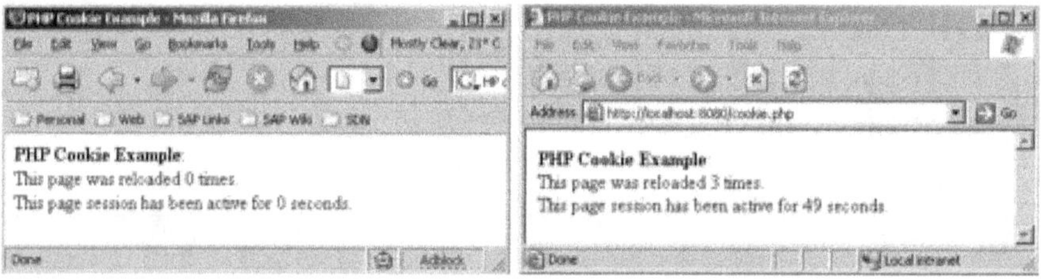

Figure 6.4: Same Page Loaded in Two Separate Browsers Showing Two Separate Kinds of Cookie Information

As you can see, the cookie is easy to implement and for users on the same machine, there really is no problem. It's very easy to implement a login that stores all the initial data from a basic login page to a cookie and then just re-read the data each time our *index.php* loads. However, problems can arise if a user closes his or her browser window, or worse, if cookies, which is something that can be configured in the browser settings, are not allowed by that user; it also means that the data is sent across with the rest of the HTTP request.

Sessions

Sessions are basically a way of storing the same data from the cookie onto the server. With each request to the server, a session ID is sent and the server is then able to match the session ID and give the application access to the data once again. This has many benefits, but it also has a few drawbacks, the main one being the possible threat of dormant sessions. *Dormant sessions* are sessions that have not been cleaned up, that is, the server doesn't know whether or not the user is still there, for example, perhaps the user went to lunch or a meeting and left his or her browser open. Because the user is no longer active in the browser, the server has no way of knowing what is going on with that session ID. Typically, the user's session is still active. To address this problem, a timeout must be set so old sessions are cleaned up and removed. With the release of PHP 4, Session Management is now available so we can use it here in our examples as well. If you remember during our installation of PHP (see Section 2.3, Installing PHP) we set a directory location for session data, so we should be able to simply start using the functions that are available with Session Management.

Create a new page under your *htdocs* directory called *session.php* and then add Listing 6.2.

Save and load this page in your browser.

```
<?php

// Initialize or reconnect to a session

session_start();

// If this new then count won't be set

// or registered

if (!session_is_registered("count")) {

session_register("count");

session_register("start");

$count = 0;

$start = time();

} else {
```

```
$count++;

}

$sessionId = session_id();

$life = time() - $start;

?>

<!DOCTYPE HTML PUBLIC "-//W3C//DTD HTML 4.0
Transitional//EN" "http://
www.w3.org/TR/html4/loose.dtd" >

<html>

<head>

<title>PHP Session Example</title>

</head>

<body>

<b>PHP Session Example</b>:<br>    This page was
reloaded <?php echo $count ?> times.<br>

This page session has been active for <?php echo
"$life"; ?> seconds.<br>

</body>

</html>
```

Listing 6.2: Simple Session Example in PHP

Upon loading your page, you'll note that it looks basically the same (see

Figure 6.5) as it does each time you reload the page. When you load a second instance of your browser, however, you'll notice that each time you refresh the browser, the count—the number of times that the page has been loaded—will always continue to increase. With the cookie, on the other hand, we were able to see the new cookie each time in the browser window in which case it was possible to have two browser windows with the same values (see Figure 6.6).

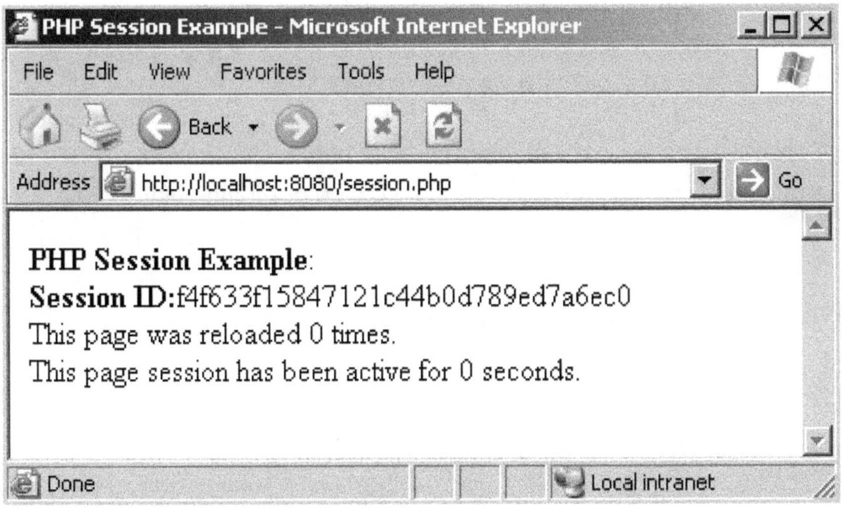

Figure 6.5: Session Example

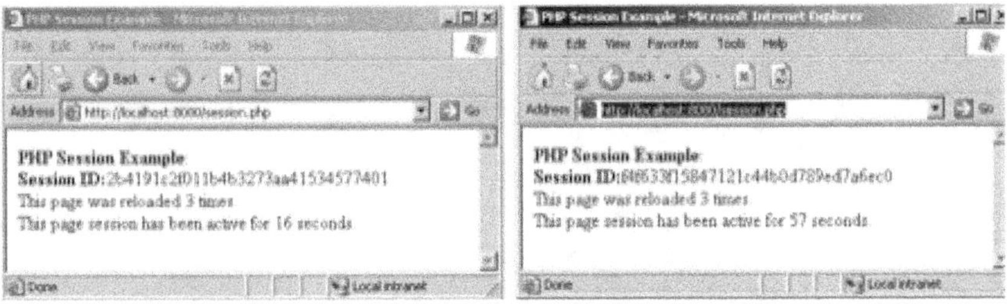

Figure 6.6: Session Example in Two Browser Instances

The reason this happens is because we called the cookie, (Remember the time stamp?), loaded the values, and then refreshed the page. With the session, we accessed the session ID each time the page was reloaded and therefore, we increased the value each time. There were two different session IDs assigned with the session. Now we can have both browsers access the same session ID. All we need to know is what the value is and request that particular session from the server.

For our new *Dynamic Login*, we will use the session and not the cookie example. In order to do this, the first item we are going to need is a login page.

Create a new PHP page in your *su01* directory called *login.php*; this is where we'll place all of our session- handling items.

Now we'll need to add Listing 6.3 to *login.php*.

Save the page, and, if you load the *login.php* in your browser, you'll see the results from Listing 6.3. This will now be our login page.

```
<?php

// Start the session management

session_start();

// Now check if the user submitted a login

if (isset($_POST['submit'])) {

$_SESSION["l_user"] = $_POST["l_user"];

$_SESSION["l_pwd"] = $_POST["l_pwd"];

$_SESSION["l_ashost"] = $_POST["l_ashost"];

$_SESSION["l_sysnr"] = $_POST["l_sysnr"];

$_SESSION["l_client"] = $_POST["l_client"];
```

```
header("Location: index.php");

}

?>

<!DOCTYPE html PUBLIC "-//W3C//DTD XHTML 1.0
Transitional//EN"
"http://www.w3.org/TR/xhtml1/DTD/xhtml1-
transitional.dtd">

<html>

<head>

<title>SU01 Transaction Login</title>

<meta http-equiv="Content-Type" content="text/html;
charset=windows-1252">

<meta name="Keywords" content="su01,user
administration,user,administration" />

<meta name="Description" content="SAP su01
transaction support in PHP" />

<meta http-equiv="pragma" content="no-cache" />

<meta http-equiv="cache-control" content="no-cache"
/>

<link rel="stylesheet" type="text/css"
href="su01.css" />

</head>

<body>

<form action="<?php echo $_SERVER['PHP_SELF']; ?>"
method="POST">

<table width="100%" cellpadding="2" cellspacing="2"
border="0">

<tr>
```

```
<td class="tb-header">SU01 Transaction Login</td>

</tr><tr>

<td align="center" valign="middle"
class="userDetail">

<table border="0" cellspacing="5" cellpadding="3">

<tr>

<td colspan="2" class="tb-header">User
Information</td>

</tr><tr>

<td>User name:</td>

<td><input type="text" name="l_user"
maxlength="30"></td>

</tr><tr>

<td>Password:</td>

<td><input type="password" name="l_pwd"
maxlength="30"></td>

</tr><tr>

<td colspan="2" class="tb-header">System
Connection</td>

</tr><tr>

<td align="right">System:</td>

<td><input type="test" name="l_ashost"
maxlength="30"></td>

</tr><tr>

<td align="right">System Number:</td>

<td><input type="test" name="l_sysnr"
```

```
maxlength="2"></td>

</tr><tr>

<td align="right">Client:</td>

<td><input type="test" name="l_client"
maxlength="3"></td>

</tr><tr>

<td colspan="2"> </td>

</tr><tr>

<td colspan="2" class="tb-header" align="center"
valign="middle">

<input type="submit" name="submit"
value="Login"></td>

</tr>

</table>

</td>

</tr>

</table>

</form>

</body>

</html>
```

Listing 6.3: Login Page Coding

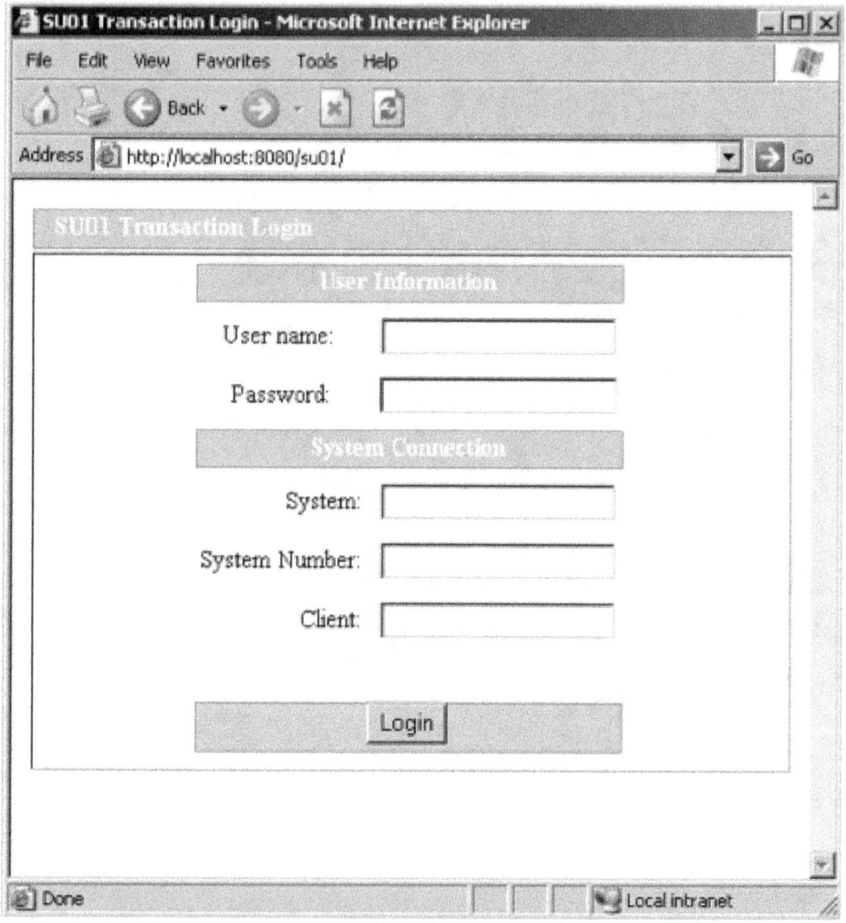

Figure 6.7:

To activate the login page automatically, we will need to make some modifications to our *index.php* page. Therefore, open this page in your editor.

To enable the session handling, we will need to start the session management. At the top of the *index.php* page, directly after “<?php”, add Listing 6.4.

```
// session initsession_start();
```

Listing 6.4: Session Management Initialization

With any login, we will need the logoff, so, add Listing 6.5 after our include ("su01.php");.

```
// Check if user chose to logoffif
(array_key_exists("action",$_GET)) {   $action =
$_GET["action"];  if ( $action == "lf" ) {
session_unset();     session_destroy();   }}
```

Listing 6.5: Catch a New Action Parameter for Logging Off

Next, we will need to replace our $sap = login line with Listing 6.6.

```
if(!isset($_SESSION["l_user"]) ||
!isset($_SESSION["l_pwd"])) {
unset($_SESSION["l_user"]);
unset($_SESSION["l_pwd"]);    header("Location:
login.php");} else {   // Now login into SAP system
$sap =
login($_SESSION["l_user"],$_SESSION["l_pwd"],$_SESSIO
N,
["l_ashost"],$_SESSION["l_sysnr"],$_SESSION["l_client
"]);
```

Listing 6.6: New Logic to Capture and Check for the Session Login Data

Don't forget to place the final "}" before "?>" to close our new IF logic statement.

Lastly, where we output our name is currently hard coded—my example shows "cmehcr1". Here we will replace "cmehcr1" with Listing 6.7, thereby making the name dynamic as well adding the **Logoff** button for the user.

```
<img src="images/s_POSITI.gif" border="0"><?php echo
$_SESSION["l_user"]; ?><a
href="index.php?action=lf"><img
src="images/s_F_CANC.gif" border="0">Logoff</a>
```

Listing 6.7: Dynamic Name and Additional Logoff Menu Option

Save your page and reload. The only physical change that you'll notice when you next log in will be displayed in the menu area (see Figure 6.8).

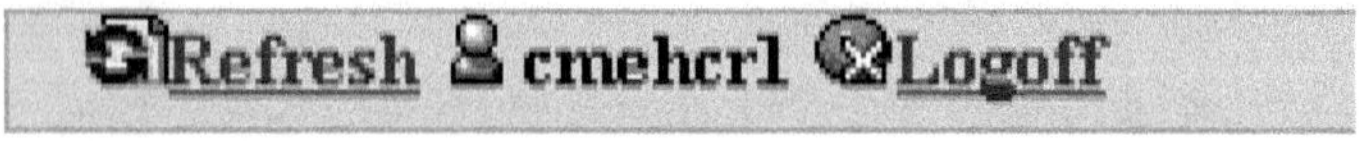

Figure 6.8: New Menu Area

You will also notice when you click on the logoff button that the page will automatically reload to the login area. This form of dynamic login will help tremendously when it comes to portability as well as working with multiple systems.

Action Log

Another area for improvement would be the action.log. After locking and unlocking users several times, the log would grow rapidly. Consequently, our first task is to ensure the log doesn't take up so much space on our page. Our second task is to be able to empty it when needed.

Better Display

It's actually quite easy to get a better display of the log; we simply need to place it within an HTML <textarea>.

Open your *index.php* file and find the spot where we output the contents of the *action.log* and replace that line with Listing 6.8.

```
<form id="actionlog">  <textarea name="actionlog"
rows="10" cols="100%">    <?php echo ShowActionLog()
?>  </textarea></form>
```

Listing 6.8: New Action Log Display

Save the file and reload your page. You'll notice that all of the text runs together.

To prevent the text from running together and consequently our not being able to read it, we will make changes to our ShowActionLog() (see Listing 6.9) and add a new line character to each line in our *action.log* file.

```
function ShowActionLog() {
$filename = "action.log";
$fp = fopen($filename, "r");
$contents = fread($fp, filesize($filename));
fclose($fp);
// Now replace any exisiting <br> tags
$contents = str_replace("<br>", "\n", $contents);
```

```
return $contents;

}
```

Listing 6.9: Replacement to ShowActionLog ( ) Function

Modifying

Now that the log file is easier to read, we see that we're missing the name of the person who performed the action. Because we can now dynamically log in to the application, this means that anyone else can log in as well. Since the *action.log* is located on the server, it will be the central log file for everyone using this application. Therefore, we now need to ensure that we add the ability to monitor who has performed an action inside the application. Finding and including this missing information is not difficult. With PHP it's very easy to modify existing functions and add new parameters.

Open *su01.php* and find the function ULUser and replace it with Listing 6.10. This will allow us to write the name of the person logged in to the log file as well.

```
function ULUser($sap,$uid,$action,$l_user) {

$value = "";

$uid = strtoupper($uid);

switch ($action) {

case "lock":

$result=$sap->callFunction("BAPI_USER_LOCK",

array( array("IMPORT","USERNAME",$uid),

array("TABLE","RETURN",array())

));

// Call successful?
```

```
if ($sap->getStatus() == SAPRFC_OK) {
// Yes, then get value
$value = $uid." has been locked by".$l_user;
} else {
// No, print long version of last error
$sap->printStatus();
}
break;
case "unlock":
$result=$sap->callFunction("BAPI_USER_UNLOCK",
array( array("IMPORT","USERNAME",$uid),
array("TABLE","RETURN",array())
));
// Call successful?
if ($sap->getStatus() == SAPRFC_OK) {
// Yes, then get value
$value = $uid." has been unlocked by".$l_user;
} else {
// No, print long version of last error
$sap->printStatus();
}
break;
}
```

```
// Now commit transaction

$result=$sap-
>callFunction("BAPI_TRANSACTION_COMMIT");

WriteActionLog($value);

}
```

Listing 6.10: Modified ULUser Function

Open *index.php* and locate where we call our ULUser function at the top of the page. Ensure that you replace the line with Listing 6.11 so you can take advantage of our new input parameter.

```
// Check if action was clicked$action = "";if

(array_key_exists("action",$_GET)) {    $action =

$_GET["action"];          if ( $action == "lock" or

$action == "unlock" ) {

ULUser($sap,$userid,$action,$_SESSION["l_user"]);

}       }
```

Listing 6.11: Modified Call to ULUser Function Showing New - Parameter

Save both files. Now, when you lock or unlock a user, you'll see your name in the *action.log* as having performed that task.

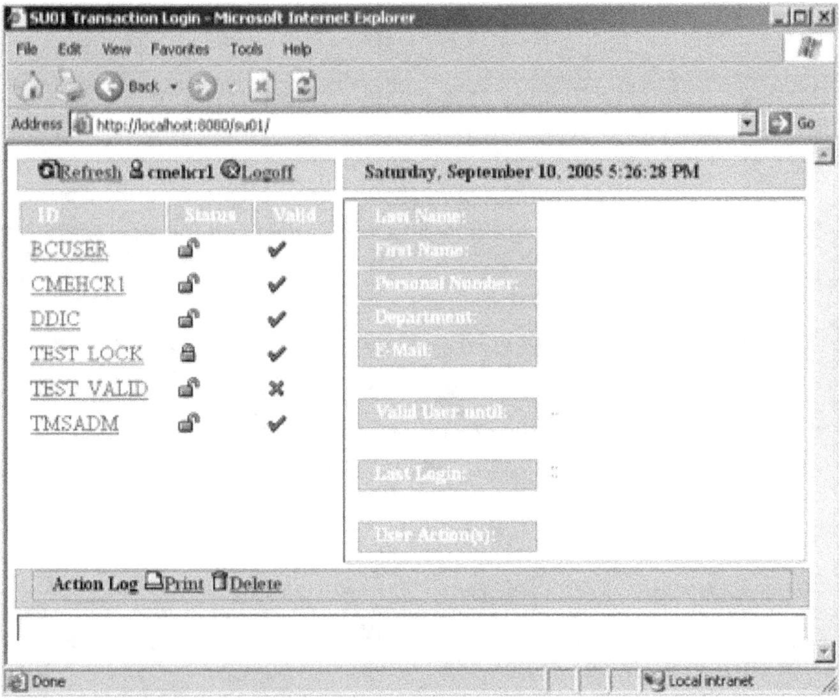

Figure 6.9: New Page Layout with All Menu Options

Deleting and Printing

Eventually, you will most likely want to empty this log so it will be easier to monitor.

Open your *index.php* file and find where we output the text "Action Log." At that spot, we will add two menu options, icons that when clicked will perform one of two actions: **Print** or **Delete** the list.

Then, add Listing 6.12 at that exact spot, that is, where you found the "Action Log" text.

```
<div class="userBody">  <span id="menu">    Action
Log    <a href="print.php" target="_blank">      <img
src="images/s_B_PRNT.gif" border="0">Print</a>    <a
href="index.php?action=ld">      <img
```

```
src="images/s_B_DELE.gif" border="0">Delete</a>
</span></div>
```

Listing 6.12: New Action Log Menu

Save the file. The actions are not yet in place, but the menu is there (see Figure 6.9).

Now at the top of *index.php,* we will add in the coding to make the actions work for "deleting" the log. Find out where we do the coding to determine whether or not the user is logged in. Once there, you will need to add the new command for "deleting" the log (see Listing 6.13).

```
if ( $action == "ld" ) {
DeleteActionLog($_SESSION["l_user"]);}
```

Listing 6.13: Delete Action Command

Open the *su01.php* file using your editor and copy Listing 6.14 into the file. This listing will do the actual deleting in the file by rewriting the *action.log* file with a single line stating that the log has been cleared. This is accomplished by the line $fp = fopen($filename, "w"); which is slightly different when we're writing other data to the log, because we then use an a command instead of the w (w is for "write", r is for "read," and a is for "append").

```
function DeleteActionLog($l_user) {
// First make a backup of the file
$backup = PrintActionLog();
$backup .= date('l dS \of F Y h:i:s A')." - Log
cleared by ".$l_user."<br>";
$filename = "action.log.".time();
$fp = fopen($filename, "w");
```

```
$write = fputs($fp, $backup);

fclose($fp);

$filename = "action.log";

$fp = fopen($filename, "w");

$string = date('l dS \of F Y h:i:s A')." - Log
cleared by ".$l_user."<br>";

$write = fputs($fp, $string);

fclose($fp);

}
```

Listing 6.14: Delete Function

Save the file, but, don't try the action just yet. If the log is emptied, you won't be able to try the next function, print, until you have performed a few more actions inside of the application.

You may have noticed that we have a command for "printing" in the new **Action Log** menu. It loads a new page call *print.php*, which you will need to create in your *su01* directory.

Add Listing 6.15 to the page.

```
<?php

include("su01.php");

?>

<!DOCTYPE html PUBLIC "-//W3C//DTD XHTML 1.0
Transitional//EN" ¬

"http://www.w3.org/TR/xhtml1/DTD/xhtml1-
transitional.dtd">

<html>

<head>
```

```
<title>Transaction SU01 - Action Log</title>

<meta http-equiv="Content-Type" content="text/html;
charset=windows-1252">

<meta name="Keywords" content="SU01,user
administration,user,administration" />

<meta name="Description" content="SAP SU01
transaction support in PHP" />

<meta http-equiv="pragma" content="no-cache" />

<meta http-equiv="cache-control" content="no-cache"
/>

<link rel="stylesheet" type="text/css"
href="su01.css" />

</head>

<body>

<table border="0" cellpadding="2" cellspacing="2"
width="100%">

<tr>

<td class="tb-header">SU01 Transaction Action Log</a>

</tr><tr>

<td><?php echo PrintActionLog() ?></td>

</tr>

</table>

</body>

</html>
```

Listing 1.15: print.php Coding

Next, add Listing 6.16 into *su01.php* and save the

```
file.

function PrintActionLog() {  $filename =
"action.log";  $fp = fopen($filename, "r");
$contents = fread($fp, filesize($filename));
fclose($fp);  return $contents;}
```

Listing 6.16: Print Function

Save the page and try “printing” your action log. Then, try “deleting” your action log.

Modify Data

The last improvement that will make our application more robust is having the ability to modify more than just whether the user is locked or unlocked. In a more large-scale application, you could recreate all of the features and functionalities of a transaction within the SAP system in a web environment.

SAPRFC makes this process quite easy for us by providing us with a code generator. If you load the *saprfc_test.php*, which is located in the SAPRFC directory, you will be able to log into your system, select your function key in your data (see Figure 6.10), and choose the -**Generate PHP** button (see Figure 6.11) having created a PHP file filled with the code necessary to achieve your goal.

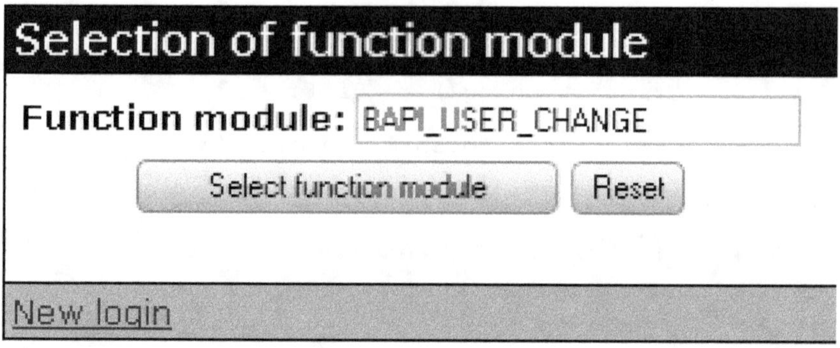

Figure 6.10: saprfc_test.php Function Select

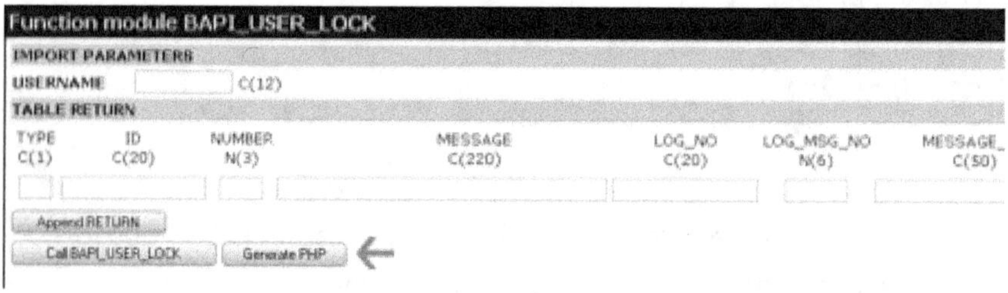

Figure 6.11: saprfc_test.php Function Example

One thing to remember when using this function is that you will need to input the codepage of your system as well.

In our example, we are going to add the ability to change the "Valid To" date in the system. It's easy and we will see an immediate change in our user list if we sent the "Valid To" date to a time before the current date. We will also add this modification to our *action.log* in order to track it.

Open your *index.php* page as we will need to alter how we display the details, as well as add a new "User Action" and coding to handle it.

In the "USER DETAIL" area, replace the output of the "Valid To" date with Listing 6.17 (see Figure 6.12). This will enable us to enter data in a field instead of just reading output.

```
<tr>  <td class="tb-header">Valid User until:</td>
```

```
<td class="tb-data">    <input type="text"
name="u_gltgb" value="<?php echo substr($userlogon¬
["GLTGB"],0,4) ?>.<?php echo
substr($userlogon["GLTGB"],4,2) ?>.<?php ¬      echo
substr($userlogon["GLTGB"],6,2) ?>">  </td></tr>
```

Listing 6.17: Modified "USER DETAIL" placeholder

Now find where we have the actions for "locking" and "unlocking" a user. Add Listing 6.18 at this spot (see Figure 6.13).

```
if ( $action == "save" ) {
SaveUser($sap,$userid,$_POST["u_gltgb"],$_SESSION["l_
user"]);}
```

Listing 6.18: New Action Item Coding

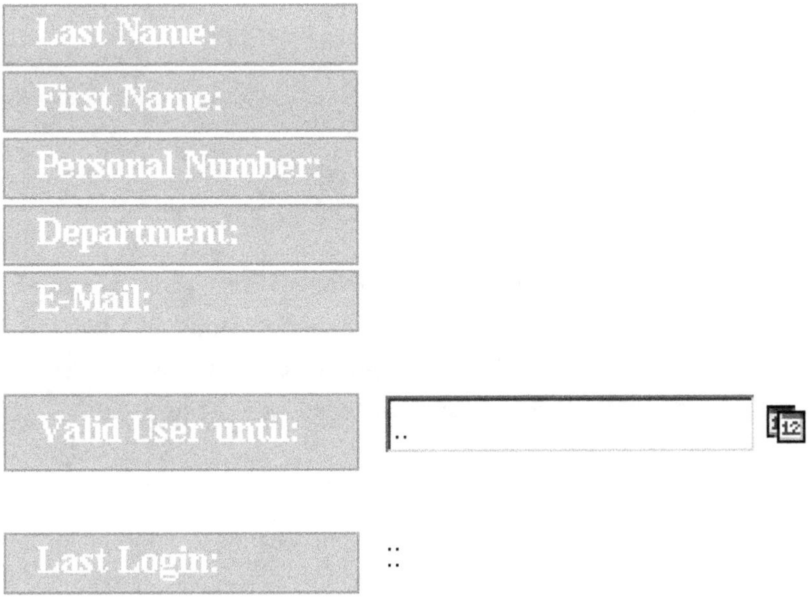

Figure 6.12: New User Details

Figure 6.13: New index.php Layout

Before the </head> tag, add Listing 6.19, which will be our JavaScript function to activate this new command.

```
<script language="JavaScript1.2"
type="text/javascript">

function SaveUser() {

userdetails.action.value = "save";

// Uncomment, remove the // from the next line to see
how to debug JavaScript

//alert("User:" + userdetails.user.value);

userdetails.submit();

}

</script>
```

Listing 6.19: JavaScript to Activate New Command

While we are in the file, let’s also change how we call each user when “locking” and “unlocking.” To do this, we need to modify the two lines that call the action, and add two new JavaScript functions (see Listing 6.20) similar to the JavaScript function above (see Listing 6.19).

```
function LockUnlockUser(whatAction) {

userdetails.action.value = whatAction;

userdetails.submit();}
```

Listing 6.20: JavaScript Replacement Commands for Locking and Unlocking

This also means that we will need to change how we retrieve the userid as well. Instead of using $_GET, we will need to access $_POST. This removes all the clutter in the URL. At the top of the page, locate where we read the "user" parameter and replace it with Listing 6.21.

```
// Check for the visible URL and then for // the POST
variablesif (array_key_exists("user",$_GET)) {
$userid = $_GET["user"];} else if
(array_key_exists("user",$_POST)) {            $userid
= $_POST["user"];}if ($userid != "") {
```

Listing 6.21: Replacement of Accessing the User Parameter

Now, for the same reasons that we changed the way in which we access our user parameter, we will add a similar replacement for accessing the action variable, namely, Listing 6.22.

```
// Check if action was clicked$action = "";// Check
for the visible URL then for the // POST variablesif
(array_key_exists("action",$_GET)) {    $action =
$_GET["action"];        } else if
(array_key_exists("action",$_POST)) {
$action = $_POST["action"];       }if ($action != "")
{
```

Listing 6.22: Replacement of Accessing the Action Parameter

In *su01.php* we will need to add our function for accessing the SAP system and storing the newly changed data, namely, Listing 6.23.

```
function SaveUser($sap,$uid,$gltgb,$l_user) {
$value = "";
```

```
$uid = strtoupper($uid);

$logondata["GLTGB"] = $gltgb;

$logondatax["GLTGB"] = "X";

$result=$sap->callFunction("BAPI_USER_CHANGE",

array( array("IMPORT","USERNAME",$uid),

array("IMPORT","LOGONDATA",$logondata),

array("IMPORT","LOGONDATAX",$logondatax)

));

// Call successful?

if ($sap->getStatus() == SAPRFC_OK) {

// Yes, then get value

$value = $uid." has been changed by ".$l_user;

} else {

// No, print long version of last error

$sap->printStatus();

}

// Now commit transaction

$result=$sap-
>callFunction("BAPI_TRANSACTION_COMMIT");

WriteActionLog($value);

}
```

Listing 1.23: PHP Function to Change User Data

```
<script language="javascript" src="scripts/cal2.js">

/*
```

```
* Source:
http://www.dynamicdrive.com/dynamicindex6/popcalendar
2.htm

*

* Xin's Popup calendar script- Xin Yang
(http://www.yxscripts.com/)

* Script featured on/available at
http://www.dynamicdrive.com/

* This notice must stay intact for use

*/

</script>

<script language="javascript"
src="scripts/cal_conf2.js"></script>
```

Listing 6.24: Implementation of the New Calendar Scripts

Save both files.

We have now completed our web page, however, there's one more modification that we can make. Often times a user will enter the date in an improper format. To address this problem, I went to *http://www.dynamicdrive.com*, and checked for their Calendar scripts and chose one that I thought would work nicely—*http://www.dynamicdrive.com/dynamicindex6/popcalendar2.htm*. Now, I just need to unpack the *.zip* file after downloading it and place the two script files in a directory under *su01* called *scripts*.

Anytime that you're using scripts found on the Internet, you must ensure that the license agreement is applicable to you and that you have the author's permission to use it in your application, especially if the application is intended for commercial use.

Add Listing 6.24 before the </head> tag in *index.php*. This is the reference to the calendar script I have chosen to use.

Then, next to the new <input type="text"> field we made in our user details, add Listing 6.25.

```
<img src="images/s_T_DATE.gif"
onclick="javascript:showCal  ('Calendar1')">
```

Listing 6.25: Clickable Image to Call the New Calendar

Then you need to modify the calendar configuration, that is, the file ***cal_conf2.js*.** Simply open it in your editor and modify it to match Listing 6.26. Here you can modify the text that the calendar uses, for example, names of the months or days of the week, and format of the output. The main change that you'll need to make is with the addCalendar line so as to ensure that your form element name and form name are correct.

```
// Define calendar(s): addCalendar ("Unique Calendar
Name", "Window title", ¬

"Form element's name", Form name")

addCalendar("Calendar1", "Select Date", "u_gltgb",
"userdetails");

// Default settings for English

// Uncomment desired lines and modify its values

// setFont("verdana", 9);

setWidth(90, 1, 15, 1);

// setColor("#cccccc", "#cccccc", "#ffffff",
"#ffffff", "#333333", "#cccccc", ¬

"#333333");

// setFontColor("#333333", "#333333", "#333333",
"#ffffff", "#333333");

// setFormat("yyyy/mm/dd");

// setSize(200, 200, -200, 16);
```

```
// setWeekDay(0);

// setMonthNames("January", "February", "March",
"April", "May", "June", "July", ¬

"August", "September", "October", "November",
"December");

// setDayNames("Sunday", "Monday", "Tuesday",
"Wednesday", "Thursday", "Friday", ¬

"Saturday");

// setLinkNames("[Close]", "[Clear]");
```

Listing 6.26: Calendar Configuration

To save some PHP processing of the date format, modify *cal2.js* and change the date format to match Listing 6.27. By removing the "/", the format is now ready for direct input into the system.

```
var calFormat = "yyyymmdd";
```

Listing 6.27: Calendar Output Format

Save both files and test the format. You may notice that you have to click on the name in the user list again in order to see the data properly changed. This is because of "when" we call the user data. Open your *index.php* file and let's modify it now.

After we locate where we output the $userlogondata and $useraddressdata variables, we'll move these two lines directly after our action calls, as shown in Listing 6.28.

```
if ($userid != "") {

// Check if action was clicked

$action = "";

// Check for the visible URL, then for the POST
variables
```

```
if (array_key_exists("action",$_GET)) {

$action = $_GET["action"];

} else if (array_key_exists("action",$_POST)) {

$action = $_POST["action"];

}

if ($action != "") {

if ( $action == "lock" or $action == "unlock" ) {

ULUser($sap,$userid,$action,$_SESSION["l_user"]);

}

if ( $action == "save" ) {

SaveUser($sap,$userid,$_POST["u_gltgb"],$_SESSION["l_
user"]);

}

}

// Now get user data

$useraddress = GetUserAddressDetails($sap,$userid);

$userlogon = GetUserLogonDetails($sap,$userid);

}
```

Listing 6.28: Rearrangement of Data Retrieval

Now save the file and let's try it again.

At this point, we have basically completed our application. We have our dynamic login, we can lock and unlock our users, we can alter their "valid to date" via typing or selecting from a calendar, and we can review all changes through our log file.

"Bells & Whistles"

Now it's time to focus on the enhancements, that is, the "Bells and Whistles," the features that don't necessarily change how the program works, just how the user sees it. These visual improvements, such as the ability to hide the "action log" or even change how much of it is displayed, can breathe life into an application and make it much easier to navigate. The last feature that we'll show you is how to modify our CSS and give the user two different displays when logging in.

By using additional Dynamic CSS and HTML, we're adding a dimension to the application, thereby giving the user a more comfortable feel for using it. A simple example to illustrate this is the calendar we already added. This small item can enhance the user's experience when using the application, as well as make using the application easier.

Hiding our Log

Let's add some code and change some areas so we can hide or show the log file. We'll have to be careful how we do this as we don't want to lose the user—who is currently being viewed in the log—in the process.

Open the *index.php* file. We'll need to make our first changes there.

What we need to add is an option for the user to click on in order to hide or show the log. The log will still be present, simply not visible if the user decides that he or she does not want to see it. We also need to add a new menu command, or, in this case, two new menu commands. These commands that are used to show or hide the log will have to be dynamic in order to display the appropriate choice based on what the user clicked, that is, a variable as well. We don't want the user to decide to hide the log when she clicks refresh, or to get the user's details for the log to reappear, therefore, we will store the user's choice in the new variable.

Find the part of the code where we show the **Print** and **Delete** (see Section 6.2, "Deleting and Printing", and Figure 6.9 above). We'll need to add some logic, so replace the two menu options with Listing 6.29. We are doing this because if the user decides to "hide" the log, we don't need to give him the options to print or delete the log. The only option that user will need is to "show" the log or to hide the log when it's visible.

```
<?php if ( $log == "sl" ) { ?>

<a href="index.php?log=hl&user=<?php echo $userid
?>"><img ¬

src="images/s_B_COLS.gif" border="0" alt="Hide
Log">Hide Log</a>

<a href="print.php" target="_blank"><img
src="images/s_B_PRNT.gif" border="0">Print</a>

<a href="index.php?action=ld"><img
src="images/s_B_DELE.gif" border="0">Delete</a>

<?php } else { ?>

<a href="index.php?log=sl&user=<?php echo $userid
?>"><img src="images/s_B_EXPA.gif" border="0"
alt="Show Log">Show Log</a>

<?php } ?>
```

Listing 6.29: New Menu Options for the Action Log

Now we also want the log to be hiding or shown, depending on the user action, so we'll need to replace where we output our log with Listing

6.30. In short, we'll be enclosing the entire table row in the code.

```
<?php if ( $log == "sl" ) { ?><tr>  <td colspan="2">
<div class="userDetail">      <form id="actionlog">
<textarea name="actionlog" rows="10" cols="100%">
<?php echo ShowActionLog() ?>        </textarea>
</form>    </div>  </td></tr><?php } ?>
```

Listing 6.30: Displaying or Hiding the Log Output

Since we have this $log variable, we also need to store it on the page for those times when the user is working or viewing the user details. Find the part of the User Details where we have

```
<input type="hidden" name="user" ¬ value="<?php echo
$userid ?>">
```

and, directly after it, add Listing 6.31.

```
<input type="hidden" name="log" value="<?php echo
$log ?>">
```

Listing 6.31: New Hidden Data Field for $log Variable

At the top of the *index.php* page, we'll need to add our logic to capture this new $log variable. Go to the top of this page and locate where we start our SAP login, right before this piece of code where we do the login, add Listing 6.32.

```
// Initialize log variable$log = "sl";if
(array_key_exists("log",$_GET)) {    $log =
$_GET["log"];} else if
(array_key_exists("log",$_POST)) {          $log =
$_POST["log"];}
```

Listing 6.32: Reading Our $log Variable from the Request

The last item for the page is to ensure that the log value stays in place when the user clicks on a person's name. To ensure that we have the right value, we will modify our user list output so as to include this new variable. Go to where we call the function <?php echo UserList($sap); ?> and replace it with Listing 6.33:

```
<?php echo UserList($sap,$log); ?>
```

Listing 6.33: Replacement to Original Line Showing New - Parameter

Save that page and open *su01.php* because we have now added a new parameter to our UserList function.

Find the function and replace it with Listing 6.34. This will update the existing function to use the new parameter.

```
function UserList($sap,$log) {

// Call function

$result=$sap->callFunction("SO_USER_LIST_READ",

array( array("IMPORT","USER_GENERIC_NAME","*"),

array("TABLE","USER_DISPLAY_TAB",array())

));

// Call successful?

if ($sap->getStatus() == SAPRFC_OK) {

// Yes, print out the user list

foreach ($result["USER_DISPLAY_TAB"] as $user) {

$user_status = GetStatus($sap,$user["SAPNAM"]);

$user_valid = GetValid($sap,$user["SAPNAM"]);
```

```
$listing .= "<tr
onMouseOver=\"this.className='highlight'\" ¬

onMouseOut=\"this.className='normal'\"><td
class=\"tb-data\">"¬

<a
href=\"index.php?log=".$log."&user=".$user["SAPNAM"].
"\">".¬

$user["SAPNAM"]."</a></td><td class=\"tb-
data\">".$user_¬

status."</td><td class=\"tb-
data\">".$user_valid."</td></tr>";

}

} else {

// No, print long version of last error

$sap->printStatus();

}

// Now return the list

return $listing;

}
```

Listing 6.34: Replacement of UserList Function

Save the file. When you reload the page, you should see the new menu option (see Figure 6.14). When clicking on the new menu option, not only should you see the log disappear, but the menu options should change as well (see Figure 6.15).

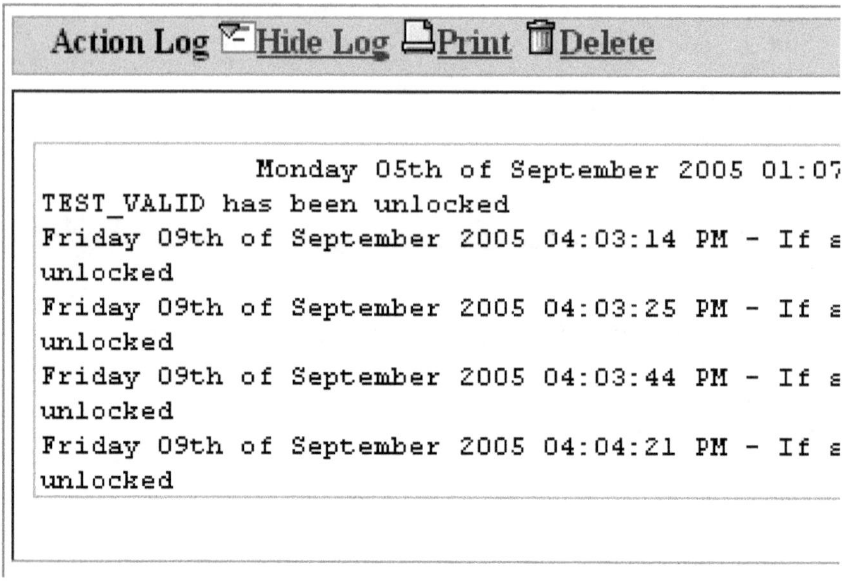

Figure 6.14: New Log Menu Options

Figure 6.15: Hiding the Log

With those changes in place, you can see that it is not exactly difficult to make small enhancements to the framework, which is an advantage of PHP being so flexible. These small enhancements can afford the user more control over his or her work, which can lead to an increase in productivity and efficiency. It is simply a matter of determining the needs of the users through feedback and interaction. I highly encourage you to solicit such feedback to better enhance the programs and applications that you develop.

Controlling the Display of Log

Another option that you can give to users is to determine how much of the log to show on the screen. With the HTML <textarea>, users can scroll, but sometimes showing more on the screen at once is helpful. To do this, we will make another change, basically, the same as the previous change. We have added another variable as well as changed the outputting.

Re-open your *index.php* file and let's work on our log menu option area again.

First, let's modify our "action log" menu again. Locate the place in the file where you added Listing 6.25, and modify it to match Listing 6.35.

Action Log

```
<?php if ( $log == "sl" ) { ?>

<a href="index.php?log=hl&rows=<?php echo $rows
?>&user=<?php echo $userid ¬

?>"><img src="images/s_B_COLS.gif" border="0"
alt="Hide Log">Hide Log</a>

<a href="print.php" target="_blank"><img
src="images/s_B_PRNT.gif" ¬

border="0">Print</a>

<a href="index.php?action=ld&rows=<?php echo $rows
?>"><img ¬
```

```
src="images/s_B_DELE.gif" border="0">Delete</a>

<?php } else { ?>

<a href="index.php?log=sl&rows=<?php echo $rows
?>&user=<?php echo $userid ¬

?>"><img src="images/s_B_EXPA.gif" border="0"
alt="Show Log">Show Log</a>

<?php } ?>
```

Log lines

```
10 <input type="radio" name="rows" value="10"
<?php if ( $rows == "10" ¬

) {?> checked <?php } ?>
onclick="ChangeRows(this.value)">

20 <input type="radio" name="rows" value="20"
<?php if ( $rows == "20" ¬

) {?> checked <?php } ?>
onclick="ChangeRows(this.value)">

30 <input type="radio" name="rows" value="30"
<?php if ( $rows == "30" ¬

) {?> checked <?php } ?>
onclick="ChangeRows(this.value)">
```

Listing 6.35: Modifications to Action Log Menu

Then, we need to add our dynamic “rows” for our HTML <textArea>. In Listing 6.30, we made modifications to this area. Now, make the additional modification by changing the “10” to “<?php echo $rows ?>”.

Next, we will add Listing 6.36 directly after where we are adding Listing 6.31. This will hold our new variable and allow us to read it again when the user refreshes the page or performs an action in the menus.

```
<input type="hidden" name="rows" value="<?php echo
$rows ?>">
```

Listing 6.36: New Hidden Form Field for Our $rows Variable

At the top of our file, we'll add our catch for the new $rows variable. So, right after you add Listing 6.28, you can add Listing 6.37. This will set the variable to a default amount and then check the request for a new value selected by the user.

```
$rows = "10";if (array_key_exists("rows",$_GET)) {

$rows = $_GET["rows"];} else if

(array_key_exists("rows",¬  $_POST)) {

$rows = $_POST["rows"];}
```

Listing 6.37: Leading the Request for Our New $rows Variable

Now we must modify our UserList function again, so you will have to add the additional parameter $rows, just as we did in Listing 6.33 for our $log *variable*.

Then, we need to make similar modifications in our *su01.php* file, just as we did in Listing 6.34 for the new $rows variable.

When we added in the part for the menu (see Listing 6.35) you probably noticed that we called a Java-Script function. We will now need to add that function (see Listing 6.38) at the top of our *index.php* page under our SaveUser function. This is the Java-Script function that will store the user-selected value indicating how many rows the user wants to display.

```
function ChangeRows(rows) {  userdetails.rows.value =

rows;  userdetails.submit();}
```

Listing 6.38: JavaScript Function for Changing the Rows of the Log

Save both files when you reload. Now, you'll see several HTML radio options next to our action log menu. The default option "10" is selected (see Figure 6.16). If you choose one of the additional options, you'll notice more of the log is displayed, that is, it's grown in size (see Figure 6.17).

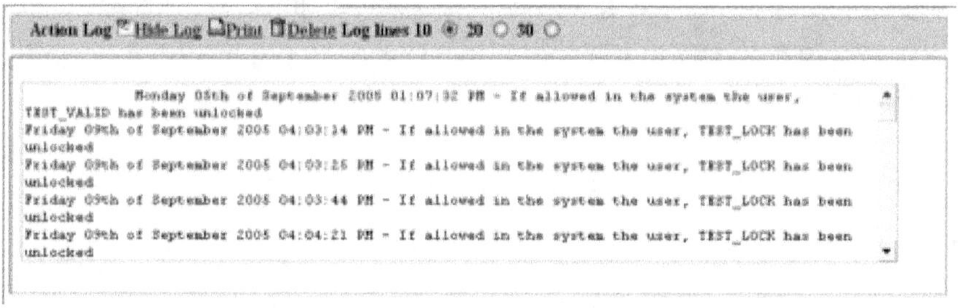

Figure 6.16: New HTML Radio Button Options for Log Size

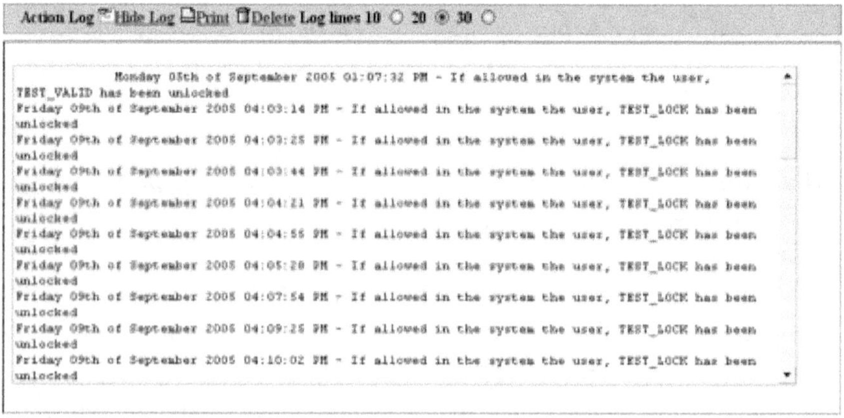

Figure 6.17: After Selecting 20 Lines Instead of 10

CSS Styles

Now that we've given the users some options, we should give them the ability to modify the page to meet their requirements. When they log in, we'll offer them two different styles to choose from, and in and the option to "invert" the color scheme while they're working with the page. For example, individuals with vision problems often have trouble dealing with certain color combinations, therefore, such an edition will make life a bit easier for them. I highly recommend that you read about "accessibility" in web applications.[1] For those of you working with SAP applications, check out the SAP Design Guild.[2]

First, we have to open our *index.php* and your *print.php* files and make some changes to handle the dynamic CSS style. This means adding a new variable and reading that variable from the session, since this happens when the user logs in.

Once we determine that the user is logged on and before we log into SAP, we need to read the $style variable (see Listing 6.39). For the *print.php* file, just add the $style variable at the top of the file, after the include.

```
// Read $style variable$style = $_SESSION["style"];
```

Listing 6.39: Reading the style Variable

If you scroll down the page into the standard HTML header area, we'll point to our style sheet now, allowing us to dynamically change the location of the external CSS file that we use to define the "look & feel" of our application. We will also move the existing style sheet and our new one to a subdirectory that you need to create called "styles." Modify the <link rel=...> line to match Listing 6.40.

```
<link rel="stylesheet" type="text/css"
href="styles/<?php echo $style ?>" />
```

Listing 6.40: Modified Line for Dynamic Styles

Save these pages and open the *login.php* file.

Before the empty row and the "submit" row in the table, we will now add Listing 6.41. This code will enable our users to choose a new existing style.

```
<tr>

<td colspan="2" class="tb-header">Theme</td>

</tr><tr>

<td colspan="2">

<select name="styles">

<option>Select a Theme

<?php

$i =1;

$css_files = array ();

$myDirectory = opendir("styles");

while ($css_file = readdir($myDirectory)) {

if (($css_file != ".") && ($css_file != "..") && ¬

!(is_dir("styles/$css_file")) && strrchr($css_file,
".") == ".css") {

$css_files[] = $css_file;

echo "<option value=\"".$css_file."\">".$css_file;

} // File is there

} // While Loop

closedir($myDirectory);

?>

</select>

</td>
```

```
</tr>
```

Listing 6.41: Dynamic Retrieval of Styles

Also add “styles/” in front of “su01.css” in the *login.php* so the login page has the default style from the start.

Now add the new styles variable to the list of session variables (see Listing 6.42).

```
$_SESSION["styles"] = $_POST["styles"];
```

Listing 6.42: New Session Variables

Save the file and load your login page. Determine whether the select option (see Figure 6.18) of style sheets is visible; most likely, only the existing *su01.css* is there. Now, if you make a copy of *su01.css*, call it *su01_blue.css*, and change all of the “lightgrey” to “#5081B2,” and then reload your login page and choose this style, you will see two different styles.

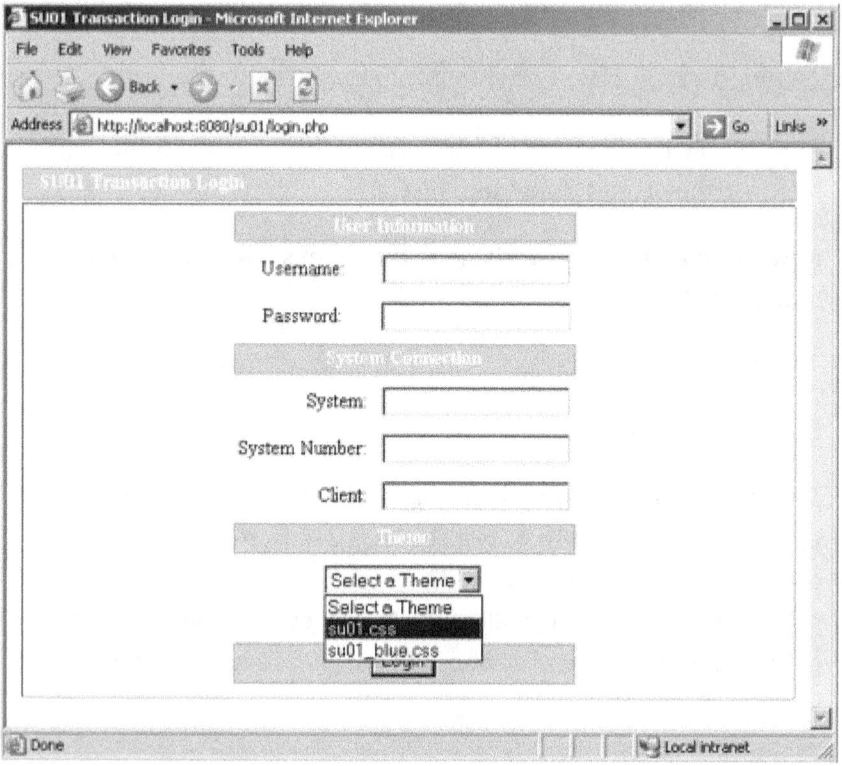

Figure 6.18: New Dynamic Styles in Login

The last CSS option that we will give to our users is the ability to invert the colors and then save this modification.

Open your *index.php* page again. We will now add an HTML checkbox to the "USER MENU" area (see Listing 6.43). You'll also need to adjust the width of the <td> for the User Menu, that is, <td width="340px">, or something similar to that.

```
 Invert Colors<input type="checkbox"
name="invert" <?php if ( $invert == "true" ) {?>
checked <?php } ?>
onclick="InvertColors(this.checked)">
```

Listing 6.43: HTML checkbox

We now need to add our JavaScript function. You can add Listing 6.44

after the SaveUser function, allowing us to store the user selection as we have previously done with the amount of rows they want to display for the log area.function Invert-Colors(value) {.

```
  userdetails.invert.value = value;
InvertColorsInitial(value);
userdetails.submit();}function
InvertColorsInitial(value) {   if ( value == "true" )
{     document.body.style.filter='invert()';
eval();   } else {     document.body.style.filter='';
eval();   }}
```

Listing 6.44: JavaScript Function for Our New HTML checkbox

After we read the request for the $rows variable at the top of our file, we'll do the same for our new $invert variable (see Listing 6.45).

```
$invert = "false";if
(array_key_exists("invert",$_GET)) {     $invert =
$_GET["invert"];} else if
(array_key_exists("invert",$_POST)) {
$invert = $_POST["invert"];}
```

Listing 6.45: Reading the Request for Our New Variable

At the bottom of the page, we will need to add Listing 6.46, just before the script for our clock. This will activate, if required, the inverted color scheme based on the user preference.

```
<script>  InvertColorsInitial¬  ('<?php echo $invert
?>');</script>
```

Listing 6.46: Activating the Script upon Loading

Add our last HTML hidden form field to hold our value (see Listing 6.47).

```
<input type="hidden" name="invert" value="<?php echo
$invert ?>">
```

Listing 6.47: HTML Hidden Form Field

Save the page and reload. The first time, you'll see the HTML checkbox and it will be unchecked (see Figure 6.19). If you check it, the change to the page will be drastic. Therefore, be careful of the colors you use in your CSS. For example, "lightgrey" is not the best choice here.

Figure 6.19: New User Menu Options

Connecting PHP to SAP HANA

For this section of the book several assumptions have been made. The first assumption is that you are already familiar with what SAP HANA is as what follows will not be an in depth or detailed description of the platform and technology. The second assumption is that you already have access to a system whether it is the trial system provided by SAP or the free developer license hosted system via one of several Cloud hosting providers. The third assumption is that you already have a basic understanding of connecting to a HANA server via the SAP HANA Studio and a working knowledge of ODATA and/or JSON, XML or ATOM.

So what is SAP HANA? Where can I find out more?

http://www.saphana.com/

http://scn.sap.com/community/developer-center/hana

SAP HANA is a completely re-imagined platform for real-time business. It transforms business by streamlining transactions, analytics, planning, predictive, sentiment data processing on a single in-memory database so business can operate in real-time. - http://www.saphana.com/community/learn, http://www.saphana.com/docs/DOC-2272

One of the best books on subject is that of the SAP HANA Essentials, http://www.saphanabook.com/, by Jeffery Word.

One of the most amazing things to happen of late was when SAP decided to create perpetual free developer licenses, http://www.zdnet.com/blog/howlett/good-news-for-sap-hana-developers-free-is-a-four-letter-word/4147, for many of their technologies and one of the first was the SAP HANA platform.

http://scn.sap.com/community/developer-center/hana

Currently at time of publishing SPS6, Revision 60 is currently available in two formats. The first is a free trial system with a 30 time period and the second is of course your very own hosted addition via one of several different Cloud providers each having different size offerings and pricing of course.

In order to explore this next section you will need to either get the 30 day trial version or your own hosted instance. Of course you will also need to setup the SAP HANA Studio and the SAP HANA Client.

There are of course multiple different scenarios one can employ when thinking of doing development with HANA and of course a common question that often comes up is which is the right one? The answer of course is the right one is the one that makes the most sense to your existing development skills and infrastructure.

What I plan to show here are some very basics and in should in way be considered a “strategy” or “decision” on how to implement PHP and HANA together it’s just a guide to help you get started.

Developer System

As I mentioned you will need your own system for this section be it either the Trial system SAP offers or your own Developer Edition on one of the hosting platforms.

As I work in regions all over the world, I will show you quickly how to get started on that platform; I recommend though that you check the SAP Developer area for the more detailed information and license information.

The process is actually quite simple; you will need to sign up for the Amazon Elastic Cloud Computing Service (EC2) and give them your credit card number. Once you have done that you will need to jump over to the service management console and select the region in which you want to work from -- I use the EU region since I am based in that reason. Once you have selected the region you will want to create a "KeyPair" this is needed when setting up your system and also if/when you need to SSH to the server.

Now that we have that taken care of you will need to "copy" your account ID and then head over to the SAP Developer area and follow the appropriate links to create your own "developer edition".

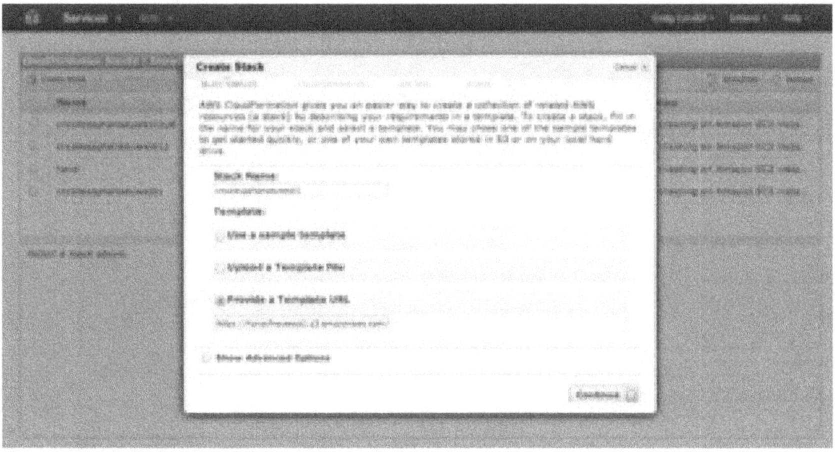

Figure 7.1: Create EC2 Stack

The link will of course launch the appropriate EC2 process with the proper template.

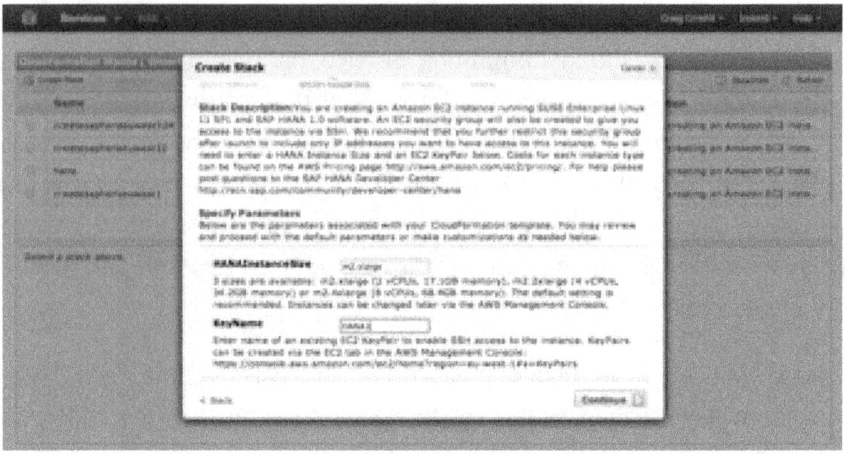

Figure 7.2: Choose system size and KeyPair

Then you will need to choose your system size and enter the KeyPair that you created.

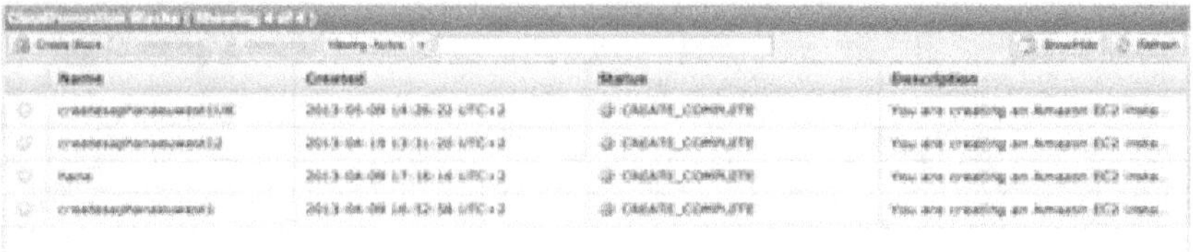

Figure 7.3: Stack Creation

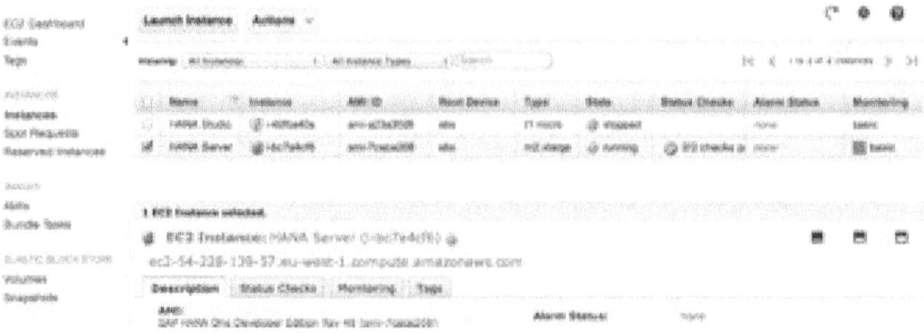

Figure 7.4: Dashboard

Once the stack has been created you will be able to see the instance starting in your EC2 Dashboard.

Now that the system is created you can either assign an Elastic IP (reserved static IP address) or just take the temporary host to add this system to your SAP HANA Studio.

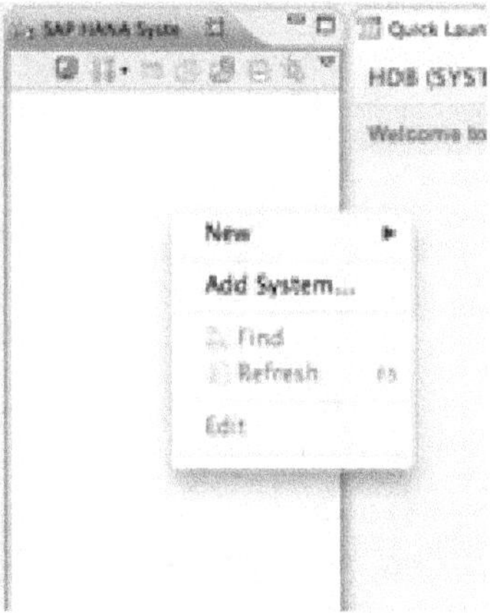

Figure 7.5: Add System in the Modeler Perspective in SAP HANA Studio

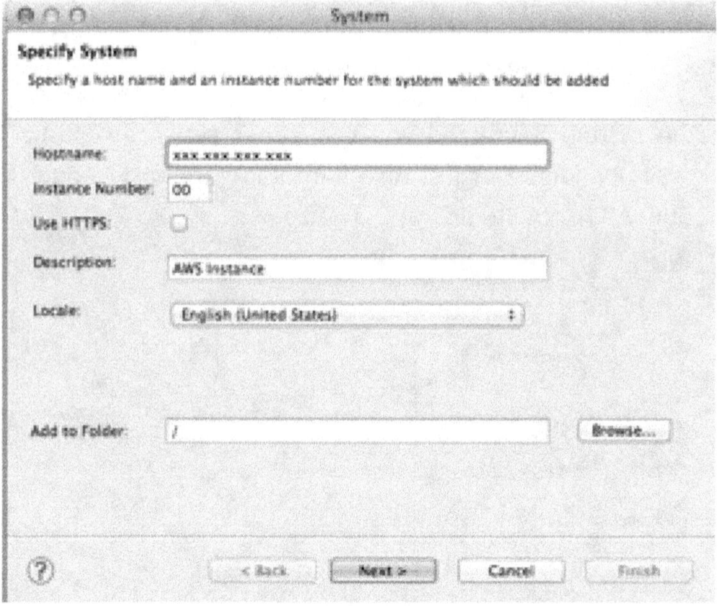

Figure 7.6: Host name, instance number and description

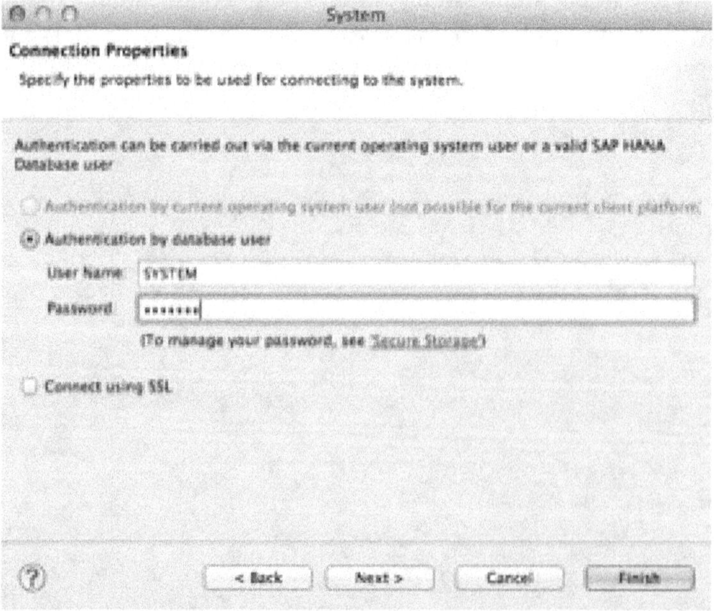

Figure 7.7: User name and password (defaults are listed in SAP Developer documents.

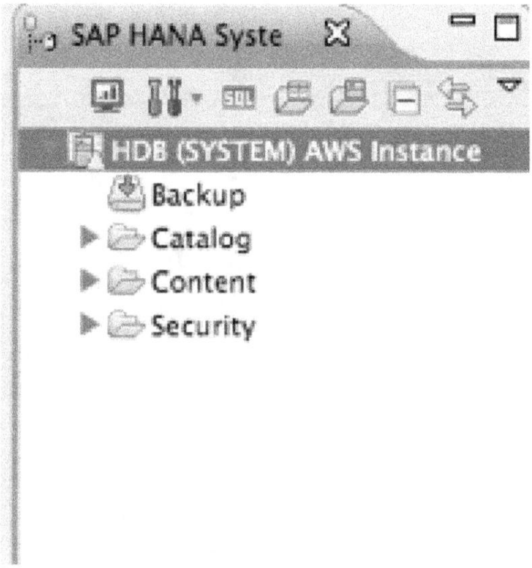

Figure 7.8: New system now accessible.

XS Project

From this point now that we have a system created and we are connected to it we are going to get some data added into it. From there we'll explore how to access that data from PHP.

There are of course two ways to add data in to a HANA system; the first is via SQL and the Catalog directly or via the repository. I'll be going the route of the repository.

First things first will be to create a new XS Project and a new SAP HANA Repository. You'll need to switch to the SAP HANA Development perspective, then add a new SAP HANA Repository which is basically a physical location for your files on your computer with a connection to the "Content" area of your SAP HANA system.

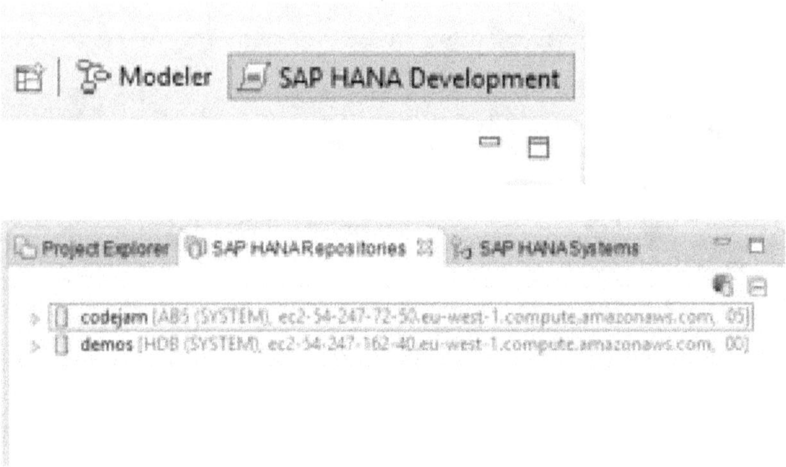

Figure 7.9: Screenshot of 2 repositories on 2 different systems.

Once you have the repository created you then switch over to your project view and create a new XS Project.

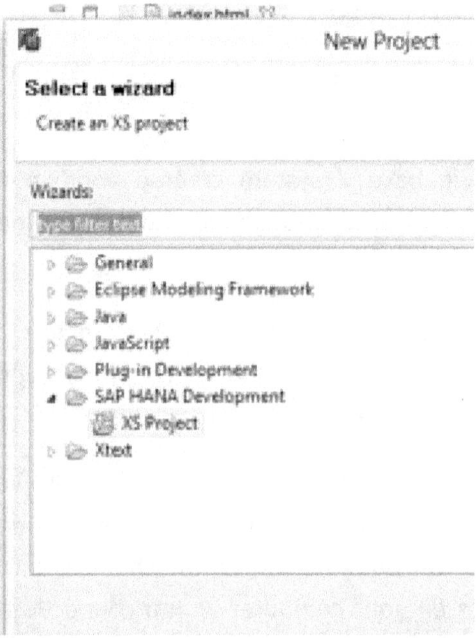

Figure 7.10: Project Wizard

I'll create a new project called "xspsa" and assign it to my "codejam" HANA repository. Then I will add 3 folders to help organize my content: "data", "services" and "ui". I'll also add the initial ".xsaccess" and ".xsapp" files required for an XS project with the basic content they require. For more information on that you can refer to the SAP HANA Development guide.

Under the "data" folder I'll be adding my table definition and my actual data to content upload upon activation.

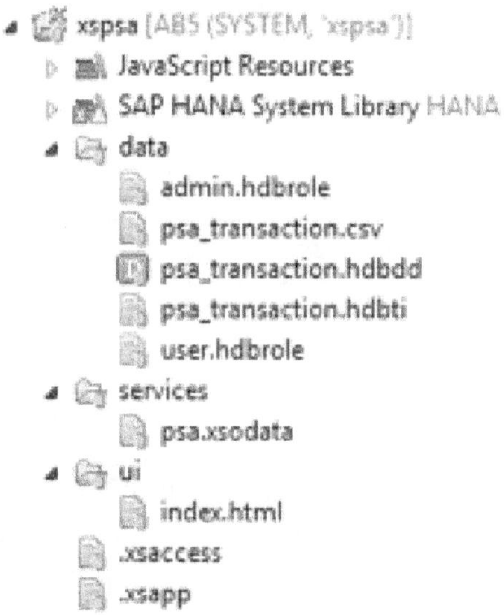

Figure 7.11: Complete Project Folder

The 3 main files in this case are the .csv file which contains CSV data for import into the table. "psa_transaction.hdbti" which is the import definition file and the actual table definition file which is "psa_transaction.hdbdd".

```
namespace xspsa.data;

@Schema: 'PSA'
context psa_transaction {
    type SString : String(40);
    type LString : String(255);
    type SDate : LocalDate;
    type AmountT: Decimal(9,3);

    @Catalog.tableType : #COLUMN
    Entity Details {
        key ID: Integer;
        AMOUNT: AmountT;
        TRAN_DATE: SDate;
        POST_DATE: SDate;
        DESCRIPTION: LString;
        CATEGORY_TEXT: LString;
    };

};
```

Figure 7.12: HDBDD file definition

Basically I define the Schema some data types and then of course the type of the table and then the actual columns of the table. Once I commit these changes to the repository and then activate the Schema will be generated, the table will be created and then the .hdbti file will do the automatic import of the CSV content to the table.

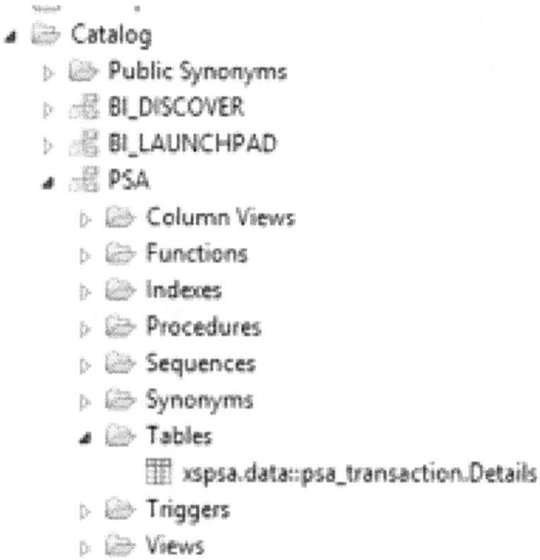

Figure 7.13: generated table from .hdbdd

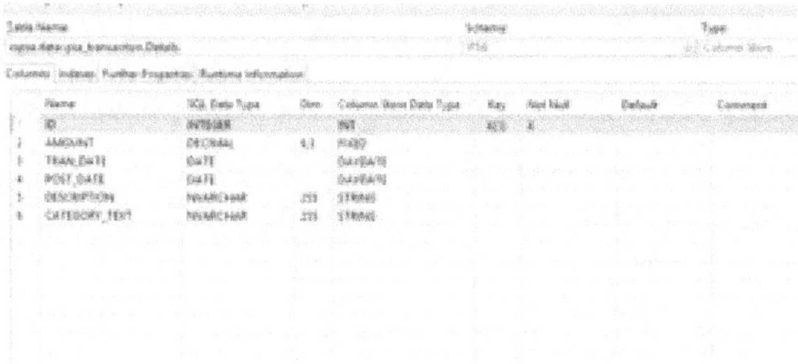

Figure 7.14: table definition

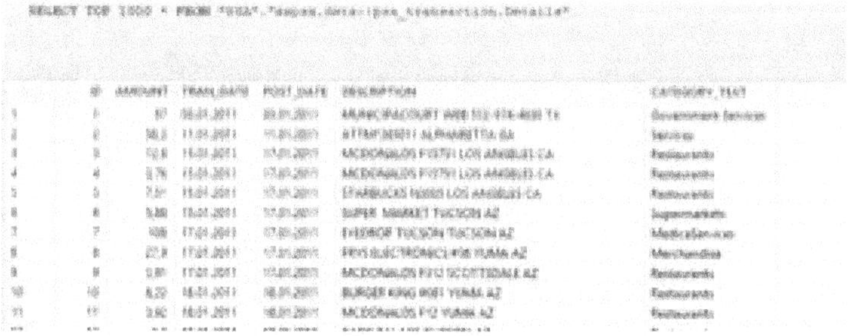

Figure 7.15: Automatically imported content

Now that we have our project and it's been activated on the server we can see under the "Content" section our new package and our files.

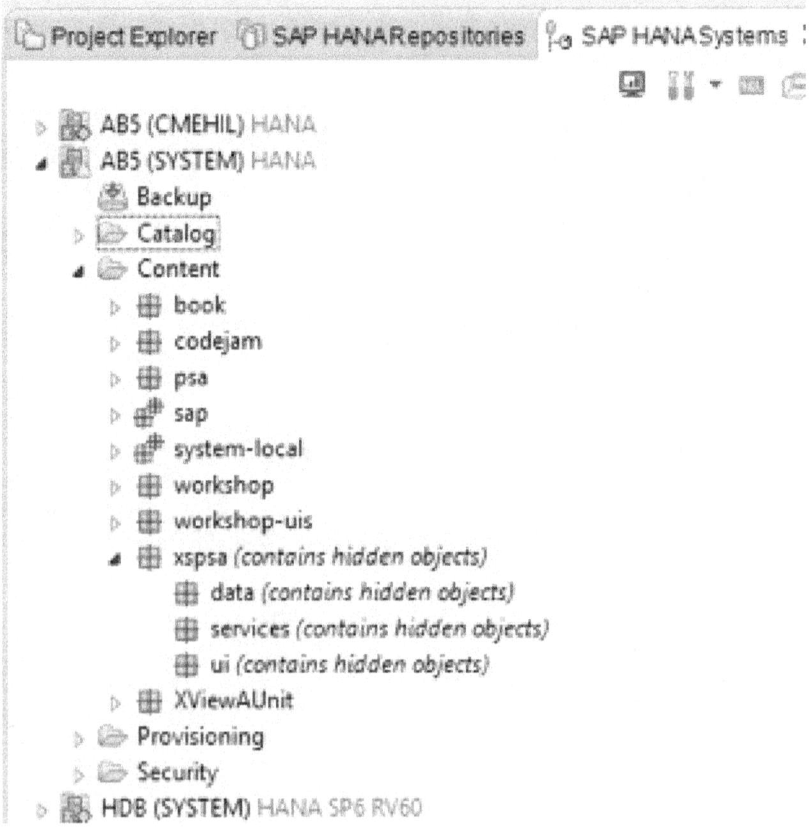

Figure 7.16: System view

Figure 7.17: Repository View

Consuming XSODATA Services

Now that we have our project created and our table with data generated let's see how easy it is to access it via a simple PHP script.

In the previous screen shots we saw under the "services" folder there was file called "psa.xsodata". This file is how we enable access via the XS engine to the table we just generated.

The content is actually extremely straight forward.

```
service namespace "codejam" {

    "PSA"."xspsa.data::psa_transaction.Details" as
"PSA";

}
```

Listing: 7.1: XSODATA format

Once we have saved that, committed it and activated it then we can try to access the data via our web browser.

http://<hostname>:80xx/xspsa/services/psa.xsodata/$metadata

Figure 7.18: Browser View

The generated service supports standard OData parameters like $metadata for introspection, $filter, $orderby, etc. It also supports body formats of ATOM/XML and JSON. Because OData is an open standard, you can read more about the URL parameters and other features at http://www.odata.org/.

We can also do a quick test from the HANA server directly using HTML and Javascript. From the previous screen shots you might have noticed the another file under the “ui” folder called index.html.

```
<!DOCTYPE HTML>

<html>
```

```
  <head>

    <meta http-equiv="X-UA-Compatible"
content="IE=edge" />

    <meta charset="UTF-8"/>

    <title>PSA OData Example SAPUI5</title>


    <script id='sap-ui-bootstrap'

        src='/sap/ui5/1/resources/sap-ui-core.js'

        data-sap-ui-theme='sap_bluecrystal'

        data-sap-ui-
libs='sap.ui.core,sap.ui.commons,sap.ui.table'>

    </script>


    <script language="JavaScript">

       var oModel = new
sap.ui.model.odata.ODataModel("/xspsa/services/psa.xs
odata/", false);

       var arrayHeaders = new Array();

       oTable = new
sap.ui.table.Table("test",{tableId: "tableID",
visibleRowCount: 10});

       oTable.placeAt("psa_table");


       //Table Column Definitions

       var oMeta = oModel.getServiceMetadata();

       var oControl;

       for ( var i = 0; i <
oMeta.dataServices.schema[0].entityType[0].property.l
ength; i++) {
```

```
            var property =
oMeta.dataServices.schema[0].entityType[0].property[i
];

            oControl = new
sap.ui.commons.TextField().bindProperty("value",prope
rty.name);

            oTable.addColumn(new
sap.ui.table.Column({label:new
sap.ui.commons.Label({text: property.name}),
template: oControl, sortProperty: property.name,
filterProperty: property.name, filterOperator:
sap.ui.model.FilterOperator.EQ, flexible: false,
width: "125px" }));

      }

      oTable.setModel(oModel);


      var sort1 = new sap.ui.model.Sorter("ID");

      oTable.bindRows("/PSA",sort1);

   </script>

</head>

<body>

   <div id="psa_table"/>

</body>

</html>
```

Listing: 7.2: XSODATA format

Using SAP UI5 this simple HTML/JavaScript code will generate a table showing the content of our database table.

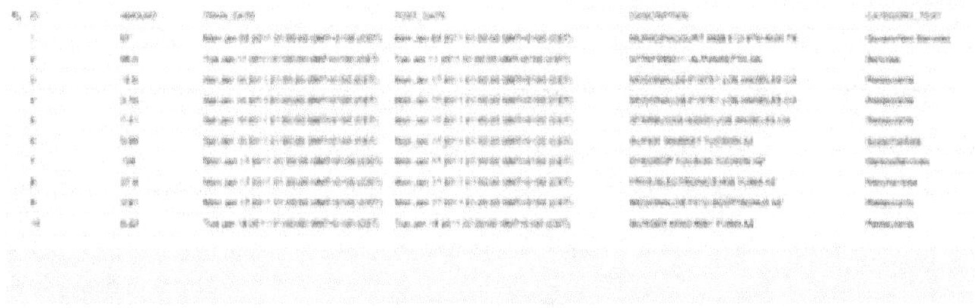

Figure 7.19: HTML SAPUI5 View

Now to see how we can access the same data via a simple PHP script. Remember unless you have setup your XS Project for "anonymous" access you'll have to account for logging in as well.

Accessing this data is as simple as doing a CURL call or a file_get_contents. It's just a matter of parsing that data as you like based on your needs.

```
$url="http://hostname:80xx/xspsa/services/psa.xsodata
/PSA/?$format=xml";

     $xml = file_get_contents($url);

    $content = simplexml_load_string($xml);


    echo "<pre>";

    print_r($content);

    echo "</pre>";
```

Listing: 7.2: XML script

This can of course be XML, JSON, ATOM or even ODATA format and you can parse the data as you need it. You can also use the SAPUI5 libraries within your PHP application and access the data via directly JavaScript calls. SAPUI5 is a JavaScript library designed by SAP and built on top of

JQUERY.

On another note, if your application is already an ODBC based application or if you need cross database compatibility. You'll need to have installed the ODBC drivers onto the server where you are executing your PHP code then it's a matter of a basic connection setting.

```
$hanaconn = odbc_connect("<SYSTEM
NAME>","<USER>","<PASSWORD>", SQL_CUR_USE_ODBC);

if (!($hanaconn)) {

 echo "<p>The connection to the HANA Serve failed: ";

 echo odbc_errormsg ($hanaconn );

 exit;

}
```

Listing: 7.3: ODBC connection

If the connection is successful at that point you can do the same basic SQL commands that you would do with other databases.

Appendix

In this Appendix, you will find complete code listings of all examples provided in this guide. Code listings include the complete listing at the different "phases" of the guide. You will also find references and the glossary.

1. Perl (also known as the Practical Extraction and Report Language) is an interpreted programming langauge designed by Larry Wall

2. Zend Technologies was founded by Zeev Suraski and Andi Gutmans in Ramat Gan, Israel.

3. See http://www.php.net/usage.php

4. The term "scripting languages" usually refers to a language that is designed to do something after an event occurs.

5. See http://sourceforge.net/projects/phpeclipse

6. Java is a development language, for more information visit http://java.sun.com

7. Eclipse is an Open Source development environment, for more information visit http://www.eclipse.org

8. Go to http://httpd.apache.org to find this project

9. On Linux installations, this is most likely a script called apachectl

10. SMTP is a protocol for sending email messages between servers. SMTP is generally used to send messages from a mail client to a mail server.

11. For Linux installations, you must stop or abort the Apache process that is running.

12. Again: On Linux installations, this is most likely a script called apachectl

13. You should note that there is an example page already provided in Section 1.3, however, I think it would be preferable to work with a page that is somewhat more familiar.

14. RFCSDK is the Remote Function Call Software Development Kit containing the necessary library (.dll files in Windows) files for working with RFC calls to the SAP System.

15. Javascript is a Client side scripting language

16. Cascading Style Sheets are design elements of a website

17. Dynamic HTML describes HTML that can alter and change once loaded in a browser window

18. For example, visit http://www.w3.org/WAI

19. See http://www.sapdesignguild.org

Chapter 5 Code

index.php

This is the initial version of our index page using a manual login.

```
<?php

        // SAPRFC class library and custom library
SU01

        require_once("saprfc.php");

        include("su01.php");
```

```
        // Now login into SAP system

        $sap = login("cmehcr1","xxxxxx");


        // Check if user name was clicked and then
retrieve user details

        $userid = "";

        $useraddress = "";

        $userlogon = "";

        if (array_key_exists("user",$_GET)) {

            $userid = $_GET["user"];

            $useraddress =
GetUserAddressDetails($sap,$userid);

            $userlogon =
GetUserLogonDetails($sap,$userid);


            // Check if action was clicked

            $action = "";

            if (array_key_exists("action",$_GET)) {

               $action = $_GET["action"];

                 if ( $action == "lock" or $action ==
"unlock" ) {

                    ULUser($sap,$userid,$action);

                 }

            }

        }
```

```
?>


<!DOCTYPE html PUBLIC "-//W3C//DTD XHTML 1.0
Transitional//EN"
"http://www.w3.org/TR/xhtml1/DTD/xhtml1-
transitional.dtd">

<html>

 <head>

   <title>SU01 Transaction</title>

   <meta http-equiv="Content-Type"
content="text/html; charset=windows-1252">

   <meta name="Keywords" content="SU01,user
administration,user,administration" />

   <meta name="Description" content="SAP SU01
transaction support in PHP" />

   <meta http-equiv="pragma" content="no-cache" />

   <meta http-equiv="cache-control" content="no-
cache" />

   <link rel="stylesheet" type="text/css"
href="su01.css" />

  </head>


 <body onLoad="goforit()">

   <table border="0" cellSpacing="2" cellPadding="2">

   <tr>

     <td>

         <div class="userBody">
```

```
          <span id="menu">

            <a href="index.php"><img
src="images/s_B_REFR.gif" border="0">Refresh</a>

              <img src="images/s_POSITI.gif"
border="0">Ccmehil

          </span>

        </div>

    </td>

    <td width="500px">

         <div class="userBody">

           <span id="clock"></span>

         </div>

    </td>

  </tr><tr>

    <td valign="top" width="120px">

      <table>

      <tr>

        <td class="tb-header">ID</td>

        <td class="tb-header">Status</td>

        <td class="tb-header">Valid</td>

      </tr>

      <?php echo UserList($sap); ?>

      </table>

    </td>
```

```
    <td valign="top" width="500px">
      <div class="userDetail">
      <table>
      <tr>
        <td class="tb-header">Last Name:</td>
        <td class="tb-data"><?php echo
$useraddress["LASTNAME"] ?></td>
      </tr><tr>
        <td class="tb-header">First Name:</td>
        <td class="tb-data"><?php echo
$useraddress["FIRSTNAME"] ?></td>
      </tr><tr>
        <td class="tb-header">Personal Number:</td>
        <td><?php echo $useraddress["PERS_NO"]
?></td>
      </tr><tr>
        <td class="tb-header">Department:</td>
        <td class="tb-data"><?php echo
$useraddress["DEPARTMENT"] ?></td>
      </tr><tr>
        <td class="tb-header">Email:</td>
        <td class="tb-data"><a href="mailto:<?php
echo $useraddress["E_MAIL"] ?>"><?php echo
$useraddress["E_MAIL"] ?></a></td>
      </tr><tr>
        <td colspan="2"> </td>
```

```
        </tr><tr>

          <td class="tb-header">Valid User until:</td>

          <td class="tb-data"><?php echo
substr($userlogon["GLTGB"],0,4) ?>.<?php echo
substr($userlogon["GLTGB"],4,2) ?>.<?php echo ¬

           substr($userlogon["GLTGB"],6,2) ?></td>

        </tr><tr>

          <td colspan="2"> </td>

        </tr><tr>

          <td class="tb-header">Last Login:</td>

          <td class="tb-data"><?php echo
substr($userlogon["LTIME"],0,2) ?>:<?php echo
substr($userlogon["LTIME"],2,2) ?>:<?php echo ¬

           substr($userlogon["LTIME"],4,2) ?></td>

        </tr><tr>

          <td colspan="2"> </td>

        </tr><tr>

          <td class="tb-header">User Action(s):</td>

          <td>

            <?php

               if (!$userid == "" ) {

                 if ( GetStatusValue($sap,$userid) ==
"UnLocked" ) {

            ?>

              <a href="index.php?user=<?php echo
$userid ?>&action=lock"><img
```

```
src="images/s_S_LOCL.gif" border="0" alt="Lock
User"></a>

           <?php } else { ?>

             <a href="index.php?user=<?php echo
$userid ?>&action=unlock"><img
src="images/s_S_LOOP.gif" border="0" alt="UnLock
User"></a>

           <?php

                }

              }

           ?>

         </td>

       </tr>

       </table>

       </div>

     </td>

   </tr><tr>

     <td colspan="2" class="tb-header">Action
Log</td>

   </tr><tr>

     <td colspan="2">

       <div class="userDetail">

        <?php echo ShowActionLog() ?>

       </div>

     </td>

   </tr>
```

```
  </table>



<script>

/*

Live Date Script - (c) Dynamic Drive
(www.dynamicdrive.com)

For full source code, installation instructions,
100's more DHTML scripts, and Terms Of Use, visit
http://www.dynamicdrive.com

*/



var dayarray=new
Array("Sunday","Monday","Tuesday","Wednesday","Thursd
ay","Friday", "Saturday")

var montharray=new
Array("January","February","March","April","May","Jun
e","July","August","September","October","November","
December")



function getthedate(){

var mydate=new Date()

var year=mydate.getYear()

if (year < 1000)

year+=1900

var day=mydate.getDay()

var month=mydate.getMonth()

var daym=mydate.getDate()
```

```
if (daym<10)

daym="0"+daym

var hours=mydate.getHours()

var minutes=mydate.getMinutes()

var seconds=mydate.getSeconds()

var dn="AM"

if (hours>=12)

dn="PM"

if (hours>12){

hours=hours-12

}

if (hours==0)

hours=12

if (minutes<=9)

minutes="0"+minutes

if (seconds<=9)

seconds="0"+seconds

// Change font size here

var cdate=dayarray[day]+", "+montharray[month]+"
"+daym+", "+year+" "+hours+":"+minutes+":"+seconds+"
"+dn

if (document.all)

document.all.clock.innerHTML=cdate

else if (document.getElementById)
```

```
document.getElementById("clock").innerHTML=cdate
else
document.write(cdate)
}
if (!document.all&&!document.getElementById)
getthedate()
function goforit(){
if (document.all||document.getElementById)
setInterval("getthedate()",1000)
}


</script>
<?php
  Logoff($sap);
?>
 </body>
</html>
```

Listing A.1 Application Using Manual Login

su01.php

This is our initial version of the page containing all of our functions.

```
<?php


function login($user,$pwd) {
```

```
        // Create SAPRFC instance

        $sap = new saprfc(array(

                        "logindata"=>array(

                        "ASHOST"=>"2.2.2.183"              //
application server

                        ,"SYSNR"=>"00"                     //
system number

                        ,"CLIENT"=>"000"                   //
client

                        ,"USER"=>$user                     //
user

                        ,"PASSWD"=>$pwd                    //
password

                        )

                        ,"show_errors"=>false              //
let class printout errors

                        ,"debug"=>false)) ;                //
detailed debugging information

                        return $sap;

}


function logoff($sap) {

        // Logoff/Close SAPRFC connection LL/2001-08

        $sap->logoff();

}
```

```
function UserList($sap) {

        // Call function

        $result=$sap-
>callFunction("SO_USER_LIST_READ",

                        array(
array("IMPORT","USER_GENERIC_NAME","*"),


array("TABLE","USER_DISPLAY_TAB",array())

                        ));



        // Call successful?

        if ($sap->getStatus() == SAPRFC_OK) {

                // Yes, print out the user list



                foreach ($result["USER_DISPLAY_TAB"] as
$user) {

                        $user_status =
GetStatus($sap,$user["SAPNAM"]);

                        $user_valid =
GetValid($sap,$user["SAPNAM"]);

                        $listing .= "<tr
onMouseOver=\"this.className='highlight'\" ¬


onMouseOut=\"this.className='normal'\"><td
class=\"tb-data\"><a
href=\"index.php?user=".$user["SAPNAM"]."\">".$user¬

                          ["SAPNAM"]."</a></td><td
class=\"tb-data\">".$user_status."</td><td
class=\"tb-data\">".$user_valid."</td></tr>";
```

```
            }


    } else {
            // No, print long version of last error
            $sap->printStatus();
    }


    // Now return the list
    return $listing;
}


function GetStatusValue($sap,$uid) {
  $value = "";
  $uid = strtoupper($uid);
  $result=$sap->callFunction("Z_GET_LOCKSTATUS",
                array(
array("IMPORT","USERNAME",$uid),

array("EXPORT","STATUS",array())
                ));
  // Call successful?
  if ($sap->getStatus() == SAPRFC_OK) {
        // Yes, then get value
        if ($result["STATUS"] == "0" ) {
```

```
            $value = "UnLocked";

          } else {

            $value = "Locked";

          }

    } else {

          // No, print long version of last error

          $sap->printStatus();

    }


    return $value;

  }


  function GetStatus($sap,$uid) {

    $value = "";


    $input = GetStatusValue($sap,$uid);

    if ($input == "UnLocked" ) {

      $value = "<img src=\"images/s_S_LOOP.gif\"
  border=\"0\" alt=\"".$input."\">";

    } else {

      $value = "<img src=\"images/s_S_LOCL.gif\"
  border=\"0\" alt=\"".$input."\">";

    }
```

```
  return $value;

}



function GetValid($sap,$uid) {

  $value = "";



  $result = GetUserLogonDetails($sap,$uid);

  $input = $result["GLTGB"];



  // Yes, then get value

  if ( strtotime("now") < strtotime($input) or $input
== "00000000" ) {

    $value = "<img src=\"images/s_S_OKAY.gif\"
border=\"0\" alt=\"".$input."\">";

  } else {

    $value = "<img src=\"images/s_S_NONO.gif\"
border=\"0\" alt=\"".$input."\">";

  }



  return $value;

}



function GetUserLogonDetails($sap,$uid) {

  $value = "";
```

```
  $uid = strtoupper($uid);
  $result=$sap->callFunction("BAPI_USER_GET_DETAIL",
              array( array("IMPORT","USERNAME",$uid),

array("EXPORT","LOGONDATA",array())
              ));
  // Call successful?
  if ($sap->getStatus() == SAPRFC_OK) {
    // Yes, then get value
    $value = $result["LOGONDATA"];
  } else {
    // No, print long version of last error
    $sap->printStatus();
  }
  return $value;
}

function GetUserAddressDetails($sap,$uid) {
  $value = "";

  $uid = strtoupper($uid);
  $result=$sap->callFunction("BAPI_USER_GET_DETAIL",
              array( array("IMPORT","USERNAME",$uid),
                     array("EXPORT","ADDRESS",array())
```

```
            ));

  // Call successful?
  if ($sap->getStatus() == SAPRFC_OK) {
    // Yes, then get value
    $value = $result["ADDRESS"];
  } else {
    // No, print long version of last error
    $sap->printStatus();
  }

  return $value;;
}

function ShowActionLog() {
  $filename = "action.log";
  $fp = fopen($filename, "r");
  $contents = fread($fp, filesize($filename));
  fclose($fp);

  return $contents;
}

function WriteActionLog($line) {
```

```
  $filename = "action.log";

  $fp = fopen($filename, "a");

  $string = date('l dS \of F Y h:i:s A')." -
".$line."<br>";

  $write = fputs($fp, $string);

  fclose($fp);

}


function ULUser($sap,$uid,$action) {

  $value = "";

  $uid = strtoupper($uid);


  switch ($action) {

    case "lock":

      $result=$sap->callFunction("BAPI_USER_LOCK",

                    array(
array("IMPORT","USERNAME",$uid),


array("TABLE","RETURN",array())

                    ));

        // Call successful?

        if ($sap->getStatus() == SAPRFC_OK) {

            // Yes, then get value

            $value = "If allowed in the system the
user, ".$uid." has been locked";
```

```
        } else {
            // No, print long version of last error
            $sap->printStatus();
        }
    break;
  case "unlock":
     $result=$sap->callFunction("BAPI_USER_UNLOCK",
                 array(
array("IMPORT","USERNAME",$uid),

array("TABLE","RETURN",array())
                 ));
      // Call successful?
      if ($sap->getStatus() == SAPRFC_OK) {
          // Yes, then get value
          $value = "If allowed in the system the
user, ".$uid." has been unlocked";
      } else {
          // No, print long version of last error
          $sap->printStatus();
      }
   break;
  }
  // Now commit transaction
  $result=$sap-
```

```
>callFunction("BAPI_TRANSACTION_COMMIT");


  WriteActionLog($value);

}


?>
```

Listing A.2 Index Page Using "Manual" Login

Chapter 6 Code

index.php

With this code sample, we now have a complete layout with all dynamic login and action log items in place.

```
<?php

        // Session init

        session_start();


        // SAPRFC class library and custom library
SU01

        require_once("saprfc.php");

        include("su01.php");


        // Check if user chose to logoff

        if (array_key_exists("action",$_GET)) {
```

```
      $action = $_GET["action"];

      if ( $action == "lf" ) {

        session_unset();

        session_destroy();

      }

    }


    if(!isset($_SESSION["l_user"]) ||
!isset($_SESSION["l_pwd"])) {

      unset($_SESSION["l_user"]);

      unset($_SESSION["l_pwd"]);

      header("Location: login.php");

    } else {

      // Now login into SAP system

      $sap =
login($_SESSION["l_user"],$_SESSION["l_pwd"],¬


$_SESSION["l_ashost"],$_SESSION["l_sysnr"],$_SESSION[
"l_client"]);


      if ( $action == "ld" ) {

        DeleteActionLog($_SESSION["l_user"]);

      }


      // Check if user name was clicked and then
retrieve user details
```

```
        $userid = "";

        $useraddress = "";

        $userlogon = "";

        // Check for the visible URL and then for
the POST variables

        if (array_key_exists("user",$_GET)) {

            $userid = $_GET["user"];

        } else if (array_key_exists("user",$_POST))
{

                    $userid = $_POST["user"];

        }


        if ($userid != "") {

            // Check if action was clicked

            $action = "";

            // Check for the visible URL then for
the POST variables

            if (array_key_exists("action",$_GET)) {

                $action = $_GET["action"];

            } else if
(array_key_exists("action",$_POST)) {

                        $action = $_POST["action"];

            }


            if ($action != "") {
```

```
                    if ( $action == "lock" or $action ==
"unlock" ) {

ULUser($sap,$userid,$action,$_SESSION["l_user"]);

                    }



                    if ( $action == "save" ) {


SaveUser($sap,$userid,$_POST["u_gltgb"],$_SESSION["l_
user"]);

                    }



                }

            // Now get user data

            $useraddress =
GetUserAddressDetails($sap,$userid);

            $userlogon =
GetUserLogonDetails($sap,$userid);



        }

    }

?>

<!DOCTYPE html PUBLIC "-//W3C//DTD XHTML 1.0
Transitional//EN"
"http://www.w3.org/TR/xhtml1/DTD/xhtml1-
transitional.dtd">

<html>
```

```
 <head>

   <title>SU01 Transaction</title>

   <meta http-equiv="Content-Type"
content="text/html; charset=windows-1252">

   <meta name="Keywords" content="SU01,user
administration,user,administration" />

   <meta name="Description" content="SAP SU01
transaction support in PHP" />

   <meta http-equiv="pragma" content="no-cache" />

   <meta http-equiv="cache-control" content="no-
cache" />


   <link rel="stylesheet" type="text/css"
href="su01.css" />


   <script language="JavaScript1.2"
type="text/javascript">


      function SaveUser() {

        userdetails.action.value = "save";

        // Uncomment,

        // remove the // from the next line to see how
to debug JavaScript

        //alert("User:" + userdetails.user.value);

        userdetails.submit();

      }
```

```
      function LockUnlockUser(whatAction) {

        userdetails.action.value = whatAction;

        userdetails.submit();

      }


    </script>


    <script language="javascript"
src="scripts/cal2.js">

    /*

     * Source:
http://www.dynamicdrive.com/dynamicindex6/popcalendar
2.htm

     *

     * Xin's Popup calendar script-  Xin Yang
(http://www.yxscripts.com/)

     * Script featured on/available at
http://www.dynamicdrive.com/

     * This notice must stay intact for use

    */

    </script>

    <script language="javascript"
src="scripts/cal_conf2.js"></script>

  </head>
```

```
 <body onLoad="goforit()">


   <table border="0" cellSpacing="2" cellPadding="2">

   <tr>

     <td>

       <div class="userBody">

         <span id="menu">

           <a href="index.php"><img
src="images/s_B_REFR.gif"  border="0">Refresh</a>

           <img src="images/s_POSITI.gif"
border="0"><?php echo $_SESSION["l_user"]; ?>

           <a href="index.php?action=lf"><img
src="images/s_F_CANC.gif" border="0">Logoff</a>

         </span>

       </div>

     </td>

     <td width="500px">

       <div class="userBody">

         <span id="clock"></span>

       </div>

     </td>

   </tr><tr>

     <td valign="top" width="120px">

       <table>

       <tr>
```

```
          <td class="tb-header">ID</td>

          <td class="tb-header">Status</td>

          <td class="tb-header">Valid</td>

        </tr>

        <?php echo UserList($sap); ?>

        </table>

      </td>

      <td valign="top" width="500px">

        <div class="userDetail">

            <form id="userdetails" name="userdetails"
method="post" action="<?php echo
$_SERVER['PHP_SELF']; ?>">

            <input type="hidden" name="user"
value="<?php echo $userid ?>">

            <input type="hidden" name="action"
value="">

            <table>

            <tr>

              <td class="tb-header">Last Name:</td>

              <td class="tb-data"><?php echo
$useraddress["LASTNAME"] ?></td>

            </tr><tr>

              <td class="tb-header">First Name:</td>

              <td class="tb-data"><?php echo
$useraddress["FIRSTNAME"] ?></td>

            </tr><tr>
```

```
                <td class="tb-header">Personal
Number:</td>

                <td><?php echo $useraddress["PERS_NO"]
?></td>

              </tr><tr>

                <td class="tb-header">Department:</td>

                <td class="tb-data"><?php echo
$useraddress["DEPARTMENT"] ?></td>

              </tr><tr>

                <td class="tb-header">Email:</td>

                <td class="tb-data"><a
href="mailto:<?php echo $useraddress["E_MAIL"]
?>"><?php echo $useraddress["E_MAIL"] ?></a></td>

              </tr><tr>

                <td colspan="2"> </td>

              </tr><tr>

                <td class="tb-header">Valid User
until:</td>

                <td class="tb-data">

                <input type="text" name="u_gltgb"
value="<?php echo substr($userlogon["GLTGB"],0,4)
?>.<?php echo ¬

                 substr($userlogon["GLTGB"],4,2)
?>.<?php echo substr($userlogon["GLTGB"],6,2) ?>">

                  <img src="images/s_T_DATE.gif"
onclick="javascript:showCal('Calendar1')">

                </td>

              </tr><tr>
```

```
          <td colspan="2"> </td>

        </tr><tr>

          <td class="tb-header">Last Login:</td>

          <td class="tb-data"><?php echo
substr($userlogon["LTIME"],0,2) ?>:<?php echo
substr($userlogon["LTIME"],2,2) ?>:<?php echo
substr($userlogon["LTIME"],4,2) ?></td>

        </tr><tr>

          <td colspan="2"> </td>

        </tr><tr>

          <td class="tb-header">User
Action(s):</td>

          <td>

            <?php

                if (!$userid == "" ) {

            ?>

                <a
href="javascript:SaveUser()"><img
src="images/s_F_SAVE.gif" border="0" alt="Save
User"></a>

            <?php

                if ( GetStatusValue($sap,$userid)
== "UnLocked" ) {

            ?>

              <a
href="javascript:LockUnlockUser('lock')"><img ¬

               src="images/s_S_LOCL.gif"
border="0" alt="Lock User"></a>
```

```
                <?php } else { ?>

                  <a
href="javascript:LockUnlockUser('unlock')"><img ¬

                   src="images/s_S_LOOP.gif"
border="0" alt="UnLock User"></a>

                <?php

                     }

                     }

                ?>

              </td>

            </tr>

            </table>

            </form>

       </div>

     </td>

   </tr><tr>

     <td colspan="2" class="tb-header">

       <div class="userBody">

         <span id="menu">

           Action Log

             <a href="print.php" target="_blank"><img
src="images/s_B_PRNT.gif" border="0">Print</a>

             <a href="index.php?action=ld"><img
src="images/s_B_DELE.gif" border="0">Delete</a>

         </span>
```

```
        </div>

      </td>

    </tr><tr>

      <td colspan="2">

        <div class="userDetail">

          <form id="actionlog">

            <textarea name="actionlog" rows="10"
cols="100%">

              <?php echo ShowActionLog() ?>

            </textarea>

          </form>

        </div>

      </td>

    </tr>

    </table>



<script>


/*

Live Date Script - (c) Dynamic Drive
(www.dynamicdrive.com)

For full source code, installation instructions,
100's more DHTML scripts, and Terms Of Use, visit
http://www.dynamicdrive.com
```

```
*/


var dayarray=new
Array("Sunday","Monday","Tuesday","Wednesday","Thursd
ay","Friday","Saturday")

var montharray=new
Array("January","February","March","April","May","Jun
e","July","August","September","October","November","
December")


function getthedate(){

var mydate=new Date()

var year=mydate.getYear()

if (year < 1000)

year+=1900

var day=mydate.getDay()

var month=mydate.getMonth()

var daym=mydate.getDate()

if (daym<10)

daym="0"+daym

var hours=mydate.getHours()

var minutes=mydate.getMinutes()

var seconds=mydate.getSeconds()

var dn="AM"

if (hours>=12)

dn="PM"
```

```
if (hours>12){

hours=hours-12

}

if (hours==0)

hours=12

if (minutes<=9)

minutes="0"+minutes

if (seconds<=9)

seconds="0"+seconds

//change font size here

var cdate=dayarray[day]+", "+montharray[month]+"
"+daym+", "+year+" "+hours+":"+minutes+":"+seconds+"
"+dn

if (document.all)

document.all.clock.innerHTML=cdate

else if (document.getElementById)

document.getElementById("clock").innerHTML=cdate

else

document.write(cdate)

}

if (!document.all&&!document.getElementById)

getthedate()

function goforit(){

if (document.all||document.getElementById)
```

```
setInterval("getthedate()",1000)

}


</script>


<?php

  logoff($sap);

?>

 </body>

</html>
```

Listing A.3   Application with Dynamic Login

su01.php

Listing A.4 shows the complete code listing for the su01.php file with all improvements for printing and deleting the action log, as well as our dynamic login.

```
<?php


function login($user,$pwd,$host,$sn,$clnt) {

       // Create SAPRFC instance

       $sap = new saprfc(array(

                    "logindata"=>array(

                    "ASHOST"=>$host           //
application server

                    ,"SYSNR"=>$sn             //
system number
```

```
                    ,"CLIENT"=>$clnt          //
client
                    ,"USER"=>$user            // user
                    ,"PASSWD"=>$pwd           //
password
                    )
                    ,"show_errors"=>false     // let
class printout errors
                    ,"debug"=>false)) ;       //
detailed debugging information
       return $sap;
}


function logoff($sap) {
       // Logoff/Close SAPRFC connection LL/2001-08
       $sap->logoff();
}


function UserList($sap) {
       // Call function
       $result=$sap-
>callFunction("SO_USER_LIST_READ",
                    array(
array("IMPORT","USER_GENERIC_NAME","*"),

array("TABLE","USER_DISPLAY_TAB",array())
```

```
                    ));

        // Call successful?
        if ($sap->getStatus() == SAPRFC_OK) {
                // Yes, print out the user list

                foreach ($result["USER_DISPLAY_TAB"] as
$user) {
                        $user_status =
GetStatus($sap,$user["SAPNAM"]);
                        $user_valid =
GetValid($sap,$user["SAPNAM"]);
                        $listing .= "<tr
onMouseOver=\"this.className='highlight'\"

onMouseOut=\"this.className='normal'\"><td
class=\"tb-data\">
                        <a
href=\"index.php?log=".$log."&user=".$user["SAPNAM"].
"\">".
                        $user["SAPNAM"]."</a></td><td
class=\"tb-data\">".$user_
                        status."</td><td class=\"tb-
data\">".$user_valid."</td></tr>";
                }

        } else {
                // No, print long version of last error
```

```
            $sap->printStatus();
      }

      // Now return the list
      return $listing;
}

function ShowActionLog() {
  $filename = "action.log";
  $fp = fopen($filename, "r");
  $contents = fread($fp, filesize($filename));
  fclose($fp);

  // Now replace any exisiting <br> tags
  $contents = str_replace("<br>", "\n", $contents);

  return $contents;
}

function PrintActionLog() {
  $filename = "action.log";
  $fp = fopen($filename, "r");
  $contents = fread($fp, filesize($filename));
```

```
  fclose($fp);


  return $contents;

}


function WriteActionLog($line) {

  $filename = "action.log";

  $fp = fopen($filename, "a");

  $string = date('l dS \of F Y h:i:s A')." -
".$line."<br>";

  $write = fputs($fp, $string);

  fclose($fp);

}


function DeleteActionLog($l_user) {

  // First make a backup of the file

  $backup = PrintActionLog();

  $backup .= date('l dS \of F Y h:i:s A')." - Log
cleared by ".$l_user."<br>";


  $filename = "action.log.".time();

  $fp = fopen($filename, "w");

  $write = fputs($fp, $backup);

  fclose($fp);
```

```
  $filename = "action.log";

  $fp = fopen($filename, "w");

  $string = date('l dS \of F Y h:i:s A')." - Log
cleared by ".$l_user."<br>";

  $write = fputs($fp, $string);

  fclose($fp);

}


function ULUser($sap,$uid,$action,$l_user) {

  $value = "";

  $uid = strtoupper($uid);


  switch ($action) {

    case "lock":

      $result=$sap->callFunction("BAPI_USER_LOCK",

                  array(
array("IMPORT","USERNAME",$uid),


array("TABLE","RETURN",array())

                  ));

        // Call successful?

        if ($sap->getStatus() == SAPRFC_OK) {

                  // Yes, then get value

                  $value = $uid." has been locked by
```

```
".$l_user;
        } else {
                 // No, print long version of last
error
                 $sap->printStatus();
        }
     break;
  case "unlock":
     $result=$sap->callFunction("BAPI_USER_UNLOCK",
                 array(
array("IMPORT","USERNAME",$uid),

array("TABLE","RETURN",array())
                 ));
        // Call successful?
        if ($sap->getStatus() == SAPRFC_OK) {
                 // Yes, then get value
                 $value = $uid." has been unlocked
by ".$l_user;
        } else {
                 // No, print long version of last
error
                 $sap->printStatus();
        }
     break;
  }
```

```
  // Now commit transaction

  $result=$sap-
>callFunction("BAPI_TRANSACTION_COMMIT");


  WriteActionLog($value);

}


function GetStatusValue($sap,$uid) {

  $value = "";

  $uid = strtoupper($uid);

  $result=$sap->callFunction("Z_GET_LOCKSTATUS",

               array(
array("IMPORT","USERNAME",$uid),


array("EXPORT","STATUS",array())

                 ));

  // Call successful?

  if ($sap->getStatus() == SAPRFC_OK) {

         // Yes, then get value

         if ($result["STATUS"] == "0" ) {

           $value = "UnLocked";

         } else {

           $value = "Locked";

         }

  } else {
```

```
          // No, print long version of last error

          $sap->printStatus();

   }


   return $value;

}


function GetStatus($sap,$uid) {

   $value = "";


   $input = GetStatusValue($sap,$uid);

   if ($input == "UnLocked" ) {

      $value = "<img src=\"images/s_S_LOOP.gif\"
border=\"0\" alt=\"".$input."\">";

   } else {

      $value = "<img src=\"images/s_S_LOCL.gif\"
border=\"0\" alt=\"".$input."\">";

   }


   return $value;

}


function GetValid($sap,$uid) {

   $value = "";
```

```
  $result = GetUserLogonDetails($sap,$uid);

  $input = $result["GLTGB"];


  // Yes, then get value

  if ( strtotime("now") < strtotime($input) or $input
== "00000000" ) {

    $value = "<img src=\"images/s_S_OKAY.gif\"
border=\"0\" alt=\"".$input."\">";

  } else {

    $value = "<img src=\"images/s_S_NONO.gif\"
border=\"0\" alt=\"".$input."\">";

  }


  return $value;

}


function GetUserAddressDetails($sap,$uid) {

  $value = "";


  $uid = strtoupper($uid);

  $result=$sap->callFunction("BAPI_USER_GET_DETAIL",

                array(
array("IMPORT","USERNAME",$uid),


array("EXPORT","ADDRESS",array())
```

```
              ));
  // Call successful?
  if ($sap->getStatus() == SAPRFC_OK) {
    // Yes, then get value
    $value = $result["ADDRESS"];
  } else {
    // No, print long version of last error
    $sap->printStatus();
  }

  return $value;;
}

function GetUserLogonDetails($sap,$uid) {
  $value = "";

  $uid = strtoupper($uid);
  $result=$sap->callFunction("BAPI_USER_GET_DETAIL",
              array(
array("IMPORT","USERNAME",$uid),

array("EXPORT","LOGONDATA",array())
              ));
  // Call successful?
```

```
  if ($sap->getStatus() == SAPRFC_OK) {
    // Yes, then get value
    $value = $result["LOGONDATA"];
  } else {
    // No, print long version of last error
    $sap->printStatus();
  }
  return $value;
}

function SaveUser($sap,$uid,$gltgb,$l_user) {
  $value = "";
  $uid = strtoupper($uid);

  $logondata["GLTGB"] = $gltgb;
  $logondatax["GLTGB"] = "X";
  $result=$sap->callFunction("BAPI_USER_CHANGE",
               array(
array("IMPORT","USERNAME",$uid),

array("IMPORT","LOGONDATA",$logondata),

array("IMPORT","LOGONDATAX",$logondatax)
               ));
```

```
  // Call successful?

  if ($sap->getStatus() == SAPRFC_OK) {

          // Yes, then get value

          $value = $uid." has been changed by
".$l_user;

  } else {

          // No, print long version of last error

          $sap->printStatus();

  }


  // Now commit transaction

  $result=$sap-
>callFunction("BAPI_TRANSACTION_COMMIT");


  WriteActionLog($value);

}


?>
```

Listing A.4 su01.php Complete Code Listing

CSS Styles Used in Our Example Application

su01.css

Listing A.5 is our complete CSS external file containing all of the CSS styles, colors, and visual settings for the entire application.

```
.userBody {
```

```
    font-size: 95%;
    font-weight: bold;
    background-color: lightgrey;
    color: white;
    border-collapse: collapse;
    border: 1px solid #aaa;
    padding: 0 .8em .3em .5em;
}

.userDetail {
    font-size: 95%;
    background-color: white;
    color: black;
    border-collapse: collapse;
    border: 1px inset #aaa;
    padding: 0 .8em .3em .5em;
}

#menu {
    font-size: 95%;
    font-weight: bold;
    line-height: 1.95em;
    background-color: lightgrey;
```

```
    color: black;

    border-collapse: collapse;

    border: 0px solid #aaa;

    padding: 0 .8em .3em .5em;

}


#clock {

    font-size: 95%;

    font-weight: bold;


    background-color: lightgrey;

    color: black;

    border-collapse: collapse;

    border: 0px solid #aaa;

    padding: 0 .8em .3em .5em;

}



.tb-header {

    font-size: 95%;

    font-weight: bold;

    background-color: lightgrey;

    color: white;
```

```
    border-collapse: collapse;
    border: 1px solid #aaa;
    padding: 0 .8em .3em .8em;
}

.tb-data {
    align: center;
    border: 0px solid #aaa;
    padding: 0 .8em .3em .5em;
}

.initial {
    background-color: #DDDDDD;
    color:#000000
}

.normal {
    background-color: #FFFFFF;
}

.highlight {
    background-color: #8888FF
}
```

Listing A.5 External CSS Style Sheet

Calendar Configuration Script

The third-party calendar configuration script I use within the application is a script that was originally located at http://www.dynamicdrive.com.

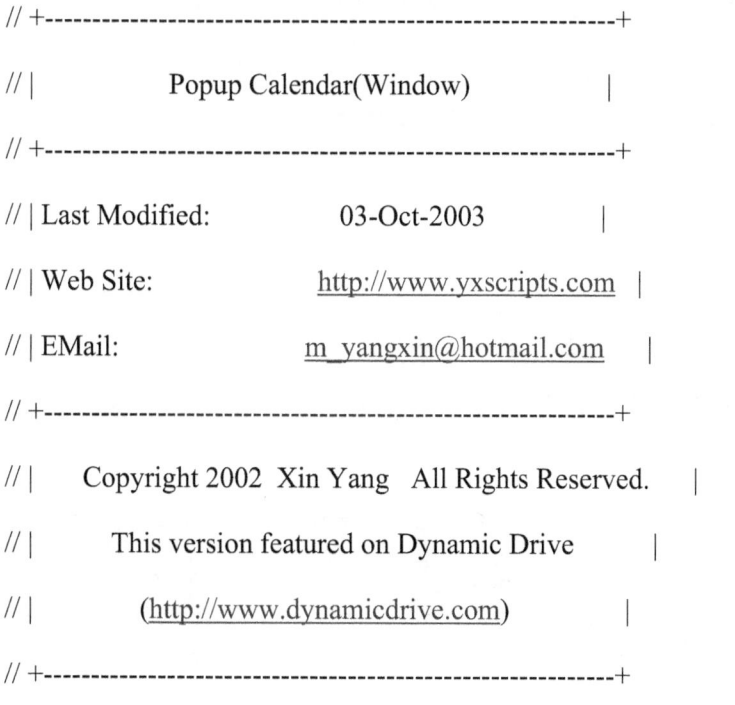

```
// +--------------------------------------------------------+
// |              Popup Calendar(Window)                    |
// +--------------------------------------------------------+
// | Last Modified:          03-Oct-2003                    |
// | Web Site:               http://www.yxscripts.com       |
// | EMail:                  m_yangxin@hotmail.com          |
// +--------------------------------------------------------+
// |     Copyright 2002  Xin Yang   All Rights Reserved.    |
// |        This version featured on Dynamic Drive          |
// |           (http://www.dynamicdrive.com)                |
// +--------------------------------------------------------+
```

Listing A.6 Copyright Notice from Third Party Calendar Script

Chapter 7 Code

index.html

```
<!DOCTYPE HTML>

<html>
```

```
  <head>

    <meta http-equiv="X-UA-Compatible"
content="IE=edge" />

    <meta charset="UTF-8"/>

    <title>PSA OData Example SAPUI5</title>



    <script id='sap-ui-bootstrap'

        src='/sap/ui5/1/resources/sap-ui-core.js'

        data-sap-ui-theme='sap_bluecrystal'

        data-sap-ui-
libs='sap.ui.core,sap.ui.commons,sap.ui.table'>

    </script>



    <script language="JavaScript">

       var oModel = new
sap.ui.model.odata.ODataModel("/xspsa/services/psa.xs
odata/", false);

       var arrayHeaders = new Array();

       oTable = new
sap.ui.table.Table("test",{tableId: "tableID",
visibleRowCount: 10});

       oTable.placeAt("psa_table");



       //Table Column Definitions

       var oMeta = oModel.getServiceMetadata();

       var oControl;
```

```
        for ( var i = 0; i <
oMeta.dataServices.schema[0].entityType[0].property.l
ength; i++) {

            var property =
oMeta.dataServices.schema[0].entityType[0].property[i
];

            oControl = new
sap.ui.commons.TextField().bindProperty("value",prope
rty.name);

            oTable.addColumn(new
sap.ui.table.Column({label:new
sap.ui.commons.Label({text: property.name}),
template: oControl, sortProperty: property.name,
filterProperty: property.name, filterOperator:
sap.ui.model.FilterOperator.EQ, flexible: false,
width: "125px" }));

        }

        oTable.setModel(oModel);



        var sort1 = new sap.ui.model.Sorter("ID");

        oTable.bindRows("/PSA",sort1);

    </script>

</head>

<body>

    <div id="psa_table"/>

</body>

</html>
```

Listing A.7   Complete SAPUI5 html code.

ABOUT THE AUTHOR

Craig is a person driven to interact and communicate, always looking to innovate over the years he's been through all spectrums of the development process for all platforms. He's built communities and helped define strategies to communicate and engage. Now though his focus has become more precise...

With a major emphasis on interaction and collaboration Craig spends a lot of time both speaking and writing about effects of social in the work place and ways to improve efficiency through the use of "social media" in the day to day work you do.

He’s been in the professional development world for almost 17 years with the last 8 within the SAP world. Within that space he’s had a chance to cross the gambit from development to strategy to marketing and communications.

www.ingramcontent.com/pod-product-compliance
Lightning Source LLC
Chambersburg PA
CBHW051454170526
45166CB00001B/240
9781493514748